THE ORIGINS OF THE SHAMANIC ASTROLOGY PARADIGM

and

INTRODUCTION TO THE SHAMANIC ASTROLOGY DIVINATION CARD DECK

by

Daniel Giamario
Illustrated by Roy Purcell

Edited by Gael Chilson

Printed in the United States of America
ISBN: 978-0-9969617-5-2
Published by *Harbingers of the Turning Of The Ages*
Interior and cover design by Rebekkah Dreskin,
blameitonrebekkah.com

Cover Art by Roy Purcell

Grandfather Rock, Wonderland of Rocks, Joshua Tree National Park
Photo by Lisa Donovan

Table of Contents

About This Book

This book is a helpful introduction to the Shamanic Astrology Paradigm and can be used with the beautifully rendered Shamanic Astrology Divination Card Deck, artfully created by Roy Purcell. It can also be used as a stand-alone introduction to the philosophical and historical foundations of the Shamanic Astrology Paradigm with the emphasis on developing greater understanding and a new foundation for masculinity and femininity. The beautifully evocative artwork of Roy Purcell provides an excellent expression of the full spectrum of the varieties of authentic masculine and feminine archetypes. It also serves to introduce the most important elements of Shamanic Astrology as represented by the full card deck.

The Shamanic Astrology Divination Card Deck has many applications:

1. The deck is a guide and divination tool for receiving intuitional guidance through a wide variety of life issues. These can include the highest of spiritual questions, as well as the most practical and mundane.

2. The deck can be used individually and collectively.

3. The deck is remarkably useful in group settings, where a circle, council, or organization can make use of its intuitive wisdom.

4. The deck can be seen as a teaching, in, and of itself, wherein the entirety and the wholeness of the Shamanic Astrology Paradigm is contained.

5. The deck is a beautiful and aesthetic work of art revealing many of the expressions of "Great Mystery."

Daniel celebrating his birthday with the Ancients.
Photo by Lynne Llamas Giamario

Author's Preface

Following my first Vision Quest experience on Mt. Shasta in 1981, during which I had my first inklings of what would become the Shamanic Astrology Paradigm, I started camping out regularly at Joshua Tree National Monument. In January of 1982, at the closest Full Moon to Epiphany, the Moon sacred to the Magi, I had an experience that changed everything for me. During that evening, at the amazing Wonderland of Rocks a special presence came alive. I heard it speak to me: "Come be with me, sit at my feet and study with me, one weekend a month for thirteen months!" I proceeded to follow those instructions over the next year, often alone and then occasionally taking small groups with me. The original ideas and framework that have developed into Shamanic Astrology and a Mystery School birthed during that time. This teacher (not in human form), whom I refer to as "Grandfather," is depicted on the front cover.

I feel so fortunate to have met Roy Purcell, synchronistically, when I needed someone to transform my visions into art. In addition to being a well-known and successful artist throughout his life, Roy has exactly the right blend of philosophical, mythological, global, and historical knowledge and experience to make this work. He shares our vision of a global synthesis that incorporates a much greater view of global humanity's true history and purpose than that which is taught and presumed known within the confines of hierarchical patriarchy and so-called "Western Civilization." Because of this, his ability to envision human potential beyond the constraints of relative cultural norms and consensus reality corresponds to the vision of the Shamanic Astrology Mystery School. I am proud to have him as a collaborator in this project.

I also want to thank the following people who have made this book and card deck possible: Cayelin Castell, co-founder of the Shamanic Astrology Mystery School, my friend and collaborator for over 20 years; Squidge Lain, who shared the vision of this deck from its inception and created the first prototype deck; Cathie Leavitt, who first experimented with possible card spreads; Erik Roth, Shamanic Astrology Mystery School Managing Director, who first discovered Roy Purcell; and especially Gael Chilson, who did the bulk of the editing, as well as creative contributions, and who also shared the vision from the beginning; also, everyone who has participated in scores of Shamanic Astrology intensives who drew the cards, as we have done as a group, at the closing circles of events.

Most special thanks to my wife and intimate life partner, Lynne Llamas, who contributed valuable feedback, shared vision, and speedy dictation. Her arrival in my life was the clearest indicator to me that the Goddess was real, and that I am loved.

Lynne Llamas and Daniel Giamario
Photo by Jim Zampathas

Lastly, I acknowledge the prior lineages and teachings that have inspired the modern developments of the Shamanic Astrology Paradigm:

*Hermes Thoth Trismegistus and Seshat, Lady of the Measuring Cord,
in originating the understanding of "As Above, So Below"*

*Imhotep, architect of the Cosmos, with the desire to have the
Earth be the mirror of Heaven*

*The Magi and all those who, throughout history, knew, like now,
when there was a great Turning Of The Ages*

The genius of the master builders of Gobekli Tepi

The Great Shining Ones at Callanish

*The knowledge and courage of the Polynesian wayfinders
traversing the great oceans*

*The astrosophy of Rudolph Steiner and the esoteric astrology of DK
and the Tibetan both presaging the Shamanic Astrology Paradigm*

*The archetypal vision of CG Jung and the cosmology
of my mentor, Dane Rudhyar*

I would also like to acknowledge my teachers that are not in human form:

Mt. Shasta

The grandfather stones at the Wonderland of Rocks

Mount Haleakala

The Fishlake Valley heirophony

The sacred landscape of Western Ireland

The author, Daniel Giamario,
in front of the site of the original transmission in January 1982,
Wonderland of Rocks, Joshua Tree National Park.
Photo by Lisa Donovan

CHAPTER ONE

The Genesis of the Project

In the *Bhagavad Gita*[1] it is written "It is better to do one's own dharma (duty), however defective it may be, than to follow the dharma of another, however well one may perform it. It is better to die doing one's own dharma, for to do the dharma of another is fraught with danger. Those who do their own dharma as their nature reveals it, never sin."[2]

Dharma means that which upholds or supports. It is also translated as duty, in the sense of natural law, or the natural order of things.

Ever since I was a little boy, I often perceived other people as if they were wearing masks. I don't mean masks in the sense of fake or false, or as in a costume. Rather, that there were certain types or varieties of people who wore the same kinds of masks and that there were a certain undetermined, but limited number of these masks. These masks were akin to a specific mold or form that different kinds of people were poured into. I always assumed that everyone saw this but never talked with anyone about it.

As I went through puberty, high school, and college in the 1960s (University of Kansas, 1966-1970), I experienced first-hand the Cultural Revolution that challenged and expanded pretty much everything in every human endeavor. Almost overnight, the extremely limited range of human possibilities expressed by consensus reality was revealed to be superficial and lacking meaning. It was very much like the movie *Pleasantville*, where the young man enters into a black and white, 1950's sitcom and slowly injects color into that world. In particular, the taught and expected roles of men and women were seldom questioned.

Conformity was so the norm that there was little possibility for even the need of a question about it.

A variety of factors conspired to create a sudden and unpredictable social change: a large middle class, dubious wars, the miraculous and unexpected effects of the Beatles, and the escalating use of marijuana and LSD which offered very different experiences than the usual drugs of choice. The astrological view attributes the change to the rare alignment of Pluto and Uranus, punctuated by Saturn and Jupiter, configurations previously seen at this intensity at the time of the French Revolution.

This is not the place for a detailed analysis of the 1960s. I, however, definitely experienced the color and diversity exploding back into the world in areas such as the political and social movements of that time, including the women's movement, Gay Liberation and the "Movement" itself, deeply questioning the role of materialism, capitalism and western civilization. There arose considerable interest in Native American and indigenous traditions at this time as well as philosophical idealism and a great deal of interest in "eastern spirituality."

At my university, the most popular professor taught Eastern Philosophy. There was a long waiting list to get into his classes and, believe it or not, the prevalent view of students was that the only major academically easier than a physical education major, was a business major; an "elitist judgment" surely, but those were the times. Liberal arts education reigned supreme. I, myself, was studying Eastern philosophy, psychology, history and East Asian studies. I actively participated in the anti-war activities and was part of a group living project known as "the Community." And yes, I gladly experimented for awhile with the psychedelic drugs that were readily available. By 1969 I had begun studying with Ram Dass and had seriously thrown myself into a variety of meditation practices, later becoming a teacher of Transcendental Meditation.

Meanwhile, Gay Liberation had arisen and the Women's Liberation Movements were full steam ahead. The Jefferson Airplane song from 1968, "Wild Thyme," expressed it perfectly: "It's a wild thyme. I see everyone around me changing faces. It's a wild thyme, I'm doing things that haven't got a name yet!"[3]

All the while, amidst this cacophony of changes, I'm still seeing the masks, the molds on the faces of my friends and still not talking about it very much. But the one thing that most stands out about those times, back when being a "hippie" simply meant to be yourself, before it was one fashion among many, was the conviction to be who you really are, separate from social or cultural conventions or expectations. Could the masks, or molds, have something to do with this?

A note here about the possible over sentimentality of what has sometimes been referred to as "being lost in the '60s." There is always the danger of sentimentality if one is nostalgically trapped in past memories and experiences. However, true "sentiment" is when the actual FEELING of a past essential experience becomes the fuel for creation in the present moment, and the current time period in history. An example of this would be the time known as the Renaissance (1450 - 1600), a "going back in order to go forward," when the rediscovery of the creative juice of an earlier time inspired and reanimated the profound leaps of progressive and creative change. The word renaissance actually means rebirth, or to be born again. The lucidity and courage of the 1960s is invoked here in that spirit.

During my last year at the University of Kansas (1969-1970), several different areas of interest converged. First, there appeared the paperback edition of an amazing book by Dane Rudhyar called *The Astrology of Personality*. This was a tour-de-force integrating history, Jungian psychology, theosophy, and spirituality, using the matrix of astrology. Up until that time, I had not been all that interested in astrology and was actually quite skeptical of it. The reading of Rudhyar's book completely opened another world for me. Rudhyar would be a mentor for me.

Not long after this, I had a girl friend who was an astrologer and I soon asked to be her "apprentice." By mid-1970 I was doing as many charts as possible for friends and pretty much anyone else who would let me!

My research into astrology, philosophy (Eastern and Phenomenology), and psychology (particularly Jungian) led me to the subject of archetypes. Originally coined in the 1540s, archetype is from the Latin, *archetypun*, from the Greek *arkhetypon*, meaning pattern or model. The adjective *arkhetpos* means "first molded," from *arkhe* meaning first and *typos* meaning model type. Also, there was the meaning of "mark of a blow." Jung used the word from 1919 onwards, meaning pervasive images appearing in consciousness as images and ideas in universal patterns present in the collective unconscious. He saw them as the basic content of religion, spirituality, mythology and art.

Related ideas conceive archetypes as the original model or type after which other similar things are patterned. The archetype can be seen as the original pattern from which copies are made. Often archetypes are perceived to speak through us. The ancients had called them the gods and goddesses. It seems that I had been seeing archetypes!

Now, I can summarize this preface by a very simple injunction, "Be your archetype." If the *Bhagavad Gita* is correct, then it is incredibly important to be authentic to your true nature even if you aren't that good at it, and to be aware that there is an actual danger if we do someone else's "dance," even if we do it perfectly. So how to know and how to practice being in alignment with your actual mold or pattern? The idealistic belief of this book is that the Universe, as "Great Mystery," is supportive of human beings who are living in accordance with their original intent, or in resonance and alignment with their original model or type that is one's archetype.

This book will offer revolutionary information describing your archetype and how to embody it in these times. The journey will use the archetypal knowledge of our authentic selves to help us by revealing the full spectrum of the archetypes (gods and goddesses) of masculinity and femininity of which there are twenty-four.

For many, the main problem is often lack of knowledge of the full spectrum of possibilities. It is difficult to be really free and co-creative with "Great Mystery" when we don't have the whole map. For example, a child, whose authentic essence is like the color purple, but is born into a family who can only see red, white, and blue, will either be seen as "wrong" or not seen at all. The map to be used is that of Shamanic Astrology. Enjoy this discovery of yourself with this diverse and comprehensive cast of characters, a veritable "round table" of gods and goddesses at this time of the *Turning Of The Ages.*

CHAPTER TWO

The Need for This Project

The need for a more comprehensive and truly practical map of human possibilities has been increasing with each year, ever since those halcyon days of the 1960s. This book is a evolutionary guide for all open-minded and inquisitive people today, particularly those who are "cultural creatives," or are soon to be.[4]

So many things are up in the air. What is a man supposed to be? What is femininity all about? What is marriage? Are human beings pair bonders? Are they polyamorous? Is the masculine a more active principle than the feminine? Is the feminine more receptive or passive? How should family be organized? When should sexual activity start? When does a person become an elder? There are many other questions like these in other aspects of life such as in politics, economics, community building, etc.

This revolutionary mapping of human possibilities at this time, circa 2015, will primarily investigate from the perspective of the individual. The system consistently reveals the most fundamental truth underlying this whole inquiry: human beings are not the same. All men are not the same. All women are not the same. This approach absolutely rejects the stereotypical "men are from Mars, women are from Venus" approach. No offense to Dr. John Gray, whose book by that name has entered these concepts into the common vernacular. There is a rich tapestry of the diversity of the archetypes of the masculine and the feminine that reflects and mirrors the diversity of our planet with its seasons and cycles.

The other main reason for the timeliness and usefulness of this mapping system is that the level of awareness and expanding capacity of cultural creatives, and other like-minded explorers, can not only handle this more complex, less simplistic typing system, but are hungering for it. But to be clear, this is not just another relationship book and not an ordinary, mainstream astrology book. Its greater ambition is to lead you, the explorer and inquirer, into your deepest longing, even beyond discovering and becoming your core archetype, your goddess or god, but towards wholeness and internal union, known here as the Sacred Marriage.[5]

THE CREATION OF MAPS

If, as our starting point, we can agree that there are archetypes, (the goddesses and gods of old), that there exists an authentic diversity of human beings, that all men are not the same and that all women are not the same, then we must explore the question, "How do we map the territory?"

There has, globally and historically, been a great diversity of approaches. As a researcher of the variety and diversity of spiritual traditions around the planet, I have always been interested in establishing the ultimate starting point. I think it is best termed "Great Mystery." This expression best captures the unnamable, unknowable "ONE REALITY," that all manifestation is part of. "Great Mystery" is how the "ONE REALITY" is referenced by the majority of indigenous and shamanically oriented cultures. It includes within it every possibility and every conception that generally occurs in the variety of religions and spiritual traditions, including monotheistic, pantheistic, polytheistic, or even atheistic ones.

Although this book is not directly about religious or spiritual mappings, or about discussing the merits or demerits of any approach, one example will be offered here as to how the mapping of the diversity of manifestation can take place.

I am reminded initially of what Martin Heidegger, the seminal German philosopher, said was the ultimate and first question, "Why is there something, rather than nothing?" So, we are assuming that manifestation has happened, as we can agree that there is, in fact, something! Now, in Hinduism, the "ONE REALITY," which we are referring to as "Great

Mystery," manifests into a trinity known as Sat Chit Ananda. Sat means pure beingness, or absolute subjectivity, or in other words, "Great Mystery" is. Chit means pure consciousness or absolute objectivity, or in other words, "Great Mystery" is aware. Ananda means pure bliss, or joy. This is the feeling of aliveness. The pure energy of "Great Mystery" that can be felt. This movement of one to three is pretty universal and is found in the Shamanic Astrology system as well.

There exists so many ways that different cultures have mapped the plan of the manifestation and unfoldment of "Great Mystery." It could be said that there are many, many ways to cut the "pie of life:"

1. The many different systems of numerology, originally inspired by Pythagoras.
2. The sixty-four hexagrams of the I Ching.
3. The fifty-two card deck, originally inspired by the cycles and seasons of this planet, sometimes referred to as the Cards of Destiny.
4. The twenty-two Major Arcane of the Tarot.
5. The wonderful system of the Enneagram, with its system of nine (three triangles) human types, which has been further developed by A.H. Almaas, to express the nine essences of human experience, namely: perfection, will, harmony, origin, omniscience, faith, plan, truth and love. From these spring other essences such as: freedom, wisdom, law, hope, transparency, strength and so on.

There is a great deal of wisdom and usefulness in each of these systems and others not referenced. In particular, many of these systems can be used oracularly, as a way of tuning into any particular moment or getting the gestalt from the mandala of a particular moment in time.[6]

While the Enneagram type systems can be extremely useful for evaluating psychological complexes and even for spiritual awakening; for many people, including me, there can be troubling levels of ambiguity as to which of the nine you actually are. As beautiful and helpful as each of these systems are, it seems as if there is always at least one elusive component missing. But what is it that is actually missing?

This brings the discussion, finally, to astrology, or "The Nightmare of Astrology," as Charles Ponce, the brilliant archetypal psychologist described it in his book, *The Game of Wizards*.

CHAPTER THREE

Astrology

"If I had ten years left to live, I would spend it studying astrology."
~ C. G. Jung

The use of astrology in this mapping system bears no relationship to the popular (or not) Sun sign astrology columns. In fact, it has nothing to do with Sun signs at all. To categorize someone by what month they were born in is somewhat better than saying all men are the same, etc., but not much. The fact that more than half of western civilization treats astrology as superstition or as simple entertainment has stemmed from the fact that Sun signs have been what astrology has been taken to be. Pretty much anyone with a modicum of intelligence or critical judgment, not to speak of actual awareness of other people, can recognize that relatively few people actually fit into their Sun sign description.

I found it interesting when I learned how this all came about. Apparently, several clever journalists in the 1800s discovered a good way to sell a newspaper column by placing the reader in a readily discernable date range. In those days, very few people had access to the information most necessary for using astrology in any meaningful way. Only a few "professionals," like a priest class or worse, someone in the black arts, had the necessary information.

Today, anyone with access to the internet or a library can easily obtain the necessary information to make this powerful mapping system immediately available. There truly is no longer any excuse to believe (or disbelieve) in Sun signs. Indeed, they shed very little light on anything of significance. As the newspaper columns say in small print, "for entertainment purposes only."

The more authentic astrology has been known, historically and globally, as the highest of the lower mysteries. By "higher mysteries" I mean the kinds of things one works toward achieving on the spiritual path including but not limited to:

1. How to experience self realization or liberation.
2. The nature of grace.
3. Entrance into the eternal now.
4. The actuality of self-love and how to develop it.

The lower mysteries include most everything in the categories of the sciences or the manifest laws of the Universe, including: physics, chemistry, astronomy, psychology, sociology, politics, economics, etc. The lower mysteries are mostly worldly, practical branches of learning, knowledge that can help human beings improve their lives and learn about the world around them. Therefore, as the highest of the lower mysteries, astrology is also the bridge and the way shower to the higher mysteries. In ancient (pre-Dark Age) times astrology was the master science, the crowning glory of all the studies leading up to it. Those were the days when astronomy and astrology were part of one study. In fact, many of the mechanistic breakthroughs in technical astronomy were developed to improve the calculations of the astrologer.

So, what are missing factors that make the other mapping systems less useful and why is authentic astrology being used for the subject matter of this book? In order to answer this question, one more issue needs to be addressed here. There is a great diversity and many varieties of astrology, globally and historically. Certainly, I am not implying that Sun sign astrology is the only kind, other than the authentic astrology I am speaking of.

There are the sidereal systems, both star-based and constellational. There are the sign based zodiacal systems, based on the earth's seasons. Additionally, there are systems based on both cycles of the Moon, sidereal and synodic. The sidereal systems include the Lunar Mansion systems of Babylonia and India. The synodic systems include the Hawaiian and other Polynesian Moon calendars, as an example.

Some astrological systems are mechanistic and deterministic, entirely based on cause and effect. For example, on a popular conversational level, we may say something like, "I can feel Saturn hitting me today." Often, this is exacerbated by the cause and effect linear nature of the English language. Many astrologers and researchers are avidly trying to find the scientific mechanism for why astrology does (or doesn't) work. There are also the ongoing debates regarding free will and determinism in the astrological community. To elaborate, some astrological approaches are quite secular, dealing exclusively with love, health and/or money. Meanwhile, many others are psychological and even fully spiritual in their orientation.

After being an astrologer for forty years, with approximately 15,000 sessions behind me and a growing school, I have developed an approach called Shamanic Astrology. This type of astrology is completely based on the ancient Hermetic dictum: "As Above, So Below, As Within, So Without," (from the *Emerald Tablet* of Hermes). It's not a cause and effect system at all. Humans are not seen as "influenced" by the planets. Rather, it's more like a set of magical correspondences.

There is, for example, an inner Saturn and an outer Saturn, the Moon within and the Moon without, and so on. In a magical and shamanic sense, they are the SAME THING. A modern analogy would be that of a hologram. No matter how small or how large, it's the same thing. There have been many times throughout history when this magical, correspondent, alchemical view was the prevalent one and not our contemporary cause and effect, scientific, linear one. These different world views change in cyclical patterns, not in a progress based, linear model. With regards to the free will/determinism question, I find it best resolved by C.G. Jung's simple and elegant statement when asked about free will. "Free will means to gladly do what you must do." In other words, they're both true and can operate together.

Another feature of Shamanic Astrology, relevant to the inquiry of this book, is that, unlike a tendency seen in the last few thousand years in astrology and much of western philosophy and religion, Shamanic Astrology honors and values the humanness of the journey of physical embodiment.

Often, there has been an inherent judgment against this world that human beings are thrown into, as if it's a lower realm of existence. Advocates of theocratic and purely evolutionary approaches long to get off the wheel of life and to ascend to higher realms, as if it is preferable to get out of this inferior realm that we must be trapped in. Esoteric Christianity often refers to our earthly incarnation as a crucifixion into matter from which one must somehow get out and get free from.

The view of Shamanic Astrology and indeed, most Shamanism, is to be grateful for our birth and amazed at the opportunity to bring spirit and consciousness into matter. This is the Journey of Involution. Rather than trying to get "off the wheel" the shamanically oriented person would more likely look forward to thousands of more lives in the only dance there is. This Journey of Involution, or spirit into matter, is the natural complement to the Journey of Evolution, or matter into spirit. As shall be explored presently, some people are more inclined to one than the other. There is no right or wrong here.

Yet another important feature of Shamanic Astrology is that it greatly facilitates the urgency to transcend the cultural overlays and unconscious assumptions and beliefs of the times. This includes the elimination of judgments of good and bad, right and wrong, high and low and better or worse. Therefore, the major tenets in more mainstream and traditional astrological knowledge have been eliminated. We won't be using words like rulership, exaltation, detriment, etc., or rating systems of strengths or weaknesses. No one is ever seen as being "Born Under a Bad Sign" as the old blues song expressed it.

Shamanic Astrology even challenges the all too often held assumptions about good or bad "karma." Under no conditions are there to be found the Christianized form of karma of rewards and punishments. Also completely eliminated is the Calvinist spin, suggesting a cruel pre-determinism, where the rich have already been rewarded for goodness and the poor have already been judged as faulty. When speaking of karma, if you look to the Indian culture that invented the concept of karma, it is often said: "Unfathomable are the ways of karma."

In fact, we are looking at a reframing of the use of astrology, so that questions like: "Is that good or is that bad?" do not even arise.

The even greater idealism that can develop from eliminating the judgments of good or bad is the creation of a framework that allows for, and supports the full spectrum of authentic human diversity. This is the "round table" of non-judgmental compassion where each place on the wheel of life is known, reinforced and supported.

So, why then astrology? More specifically, why use Shamanic Astrology to inspire our mapping? As the highest of the lower mysteries it has, historically and globally, most comprehensively included the greatest number of ingredients and features of global humanity's existence on this planet, most notably, the astronomy with the cycles and seasons of our earth in space. The specific diversity and complexity in human beings is directly linked to "As Above, So Below, As Within, So Without," to the actual physical elements of our specific earth's spin, tilt and wobble, over very specific seasons and cycles in relationship to a very specific sun and solar system and galaxy.

This comprehensive, physical knowledge is not all. Included is the vast history of humanity: political, economic, cultural, and particularly, psychological and spiritual. The cycles of human experience are also there, including the matriarchal, patriarchal, Neolithic, egalitarian, hierarchical – all of it.

Astrology reflects and illustrates the actual cosmological design. Encoded in the magical hologram of "Great Mystery," perceived as the great "As Above, So Below," are the mechanics and blueprint of how archetypes, myth and symbol change over time. Shamanic Astrology honors and includes the widest possible spectrum of authentic diversity. And since astrology is also the study of seasons and cycles, consequently, it remains organically ever changing. The archetypes (the gods and goddesses) are continuously, over the ages and epochs, dancing in new, creative ways.

There is no rigid dogma about any of this. It is all rather like the experience and endeavors of beings like the Merlin or the Priestesses of

Avalon, who had to be aware of and willing to work with three realms of experience simultaneously:

1. The knowledge, awareness and appreciation of the old ways of the previous ages that continue to have essence and value.

2. The knowledge, awareness and appreciation of new, imaginative and innovative ways that have essence and value.

3. The knowledge, awareness and appreciation for the eternal verities of essence and value that transcend any specific time period, age or epoch.

This describes the mission of the Shamanic Astrologer.

The logo of the Shamanic Astrology Mystery School showing the current alignment of constellations along the ecliptic with the signs of the zodiac.

the energy of the zodiac

sun

CHAPTER FOUR

An Individual's Place in Time

There is a specific time related to the individual person. Unlike the divinatory and mandalic systems noted before, authentic astrology specifically places the individual human being at the exact time of the first breath, representing the first instance of being separate from the biological support system of the mother. The uniqueness of that individual's life is revealed by the lunar, solar, planetary, and galactic cycles relative to that specific place on this specific planet at a specific place in time.

That time is directly referenced by when this event occurs on the solar calendar. The Sun is, of course, central, but not as in Sun sign astrology. The Sun, seen from the point of view of Shamanic Astrology, is the only thing in nature that can't be physically looked at directly for very long. It is the visible and manifest expression of "Great Mystery" itself, and without it no life on this planet would be possible. It is completely understandable that the Sun has been deified so many times by so many cultures. However, it's a mistake to project any specific archetype or symbol onto the Sun, and certainly not secular Sun sign characterizations.

Therefore, an authentic astrology, of which Shamanic Astrology is one, as the highest of the lowest mysteries, is understandably the best possible mandalic mapping system, because it most comprehensibly takes into account the whole story of place and time related to the person, hence perfect for this book's project.

But it must be said that even the best astrology will never know the whole story or final truth. In fact, the more a system like astrology is mastered, the more humbling the experience is. What astrologers and other cosmic or psychological mappers discover is that the astrologer, also, is part of the ultimately unknowable "Great Mystery" and also part of its unfolding. No complete or certain objectivity can ever be possible.

Having said that, however, I know of no better set of tools for taking responsibility in co-creating with "Great Mystery." We each have our own individual journey to align with our dharma through knowing our personal gods and goddesses. In doing so, internal wholeness can be created from which interaction with others in relationship develops from a place of authenticity and integrity.

THE JOURNEY OF THE SOUL

Before introducing the twenty-four goddesses and gods, this section describes the Shamanic Astrology view of the "Journey of the Soul"[7] and will elucidate on a deeper level the notions of intent, purpose and meaning.

Two assumptions are made in this work:

ONE: The life we live has meaning and purpose. Life is not a crapshoot of random, meaningless, purposeless events in which either there are good or bad hands or the luck of the draw. I know that many philosophers and scientists believe that it is. That is what they choose to believe.

I, however, take my cue from the French writer, Albert Camus. When faced with the nihilism and "life is absurd" views of the Sartrean existentialists, he responded as follows, to paraphrase: "Okay, let's provisionally accept your view that life is a crapshoot and you either have a good hand, or not. The purpose of existence as a human being is to rebel against the absurdity and create meaning and purpose."

This viewpoint is in harmony with Jungian psychology. In Jung's time, he was surrounded by psychologies that believed the primary human motivations were variously sex, will, power and survival. Instead, Jung believed that a deeper motivation was the quest for meaning and purpose, and I concur.

Personally, I believe there is a higher order of meaning and purpose that are partially revealed as the essential qualities of "Great Mystery." These essential qualities reveal their nature through the map of archetypes, which are an expression of natural law (dharma).

This book will layer on and elaborate additional aspects of meaning and purpose. But even if there is no higher realm of meaning or purpose, even that of natural law, human beings still have the freedom to choose to create that meaning or purpose which makes a life worth living. The gnosis, or the experience of that higher meaning, would be akin to dessert, an additional bonus to a life lived in accordance with original intent.

TWO: Upon birth, men and women are not blank slates. There are attitudes, habits, addictions, predispositions and skill sets that pre-exist prior to them being modified by parents, culture and the time of history we are born into.

This is contrary to the beliefs of "the Behaviorists," who pretty much think that who we become is entirely based upon our early life conditions.

Shamanic Astrology takes no position on how this all occurs. It could be what's written in the genetic code, it could be the family history and/or it could be some sense of past lives or some combination of these. Even if the imagery of past lives is used, it works mythically, without the necessity of literalness.

Contemporary psychologies sometimes use this "mythic" sense of past lives, to create a story or motif that helps to make sense out of and expand upon the meaning and purpose of life. Sometimes, it's called creating your personal myth. Shamanic Astrology takes the position that there is definitely an original collection of essential qualities and archetypal energies that are basic to the individual and upon which outside forces can do very little to change.

CHAPTER FIVE

The Journey

The journey of the soul can be likened to a symphony of three movements, or three acts in a play.

THE FIRST MOVEMENT

LINEAGE, coming from the word meaning your "line of descent," in Shamanic Astrology, is primarily represented by the natal position of the Moon. The twelve Moon positions are akin to twelve tribes, or twelve schools or universities. Sometimes we call them *mystery schools*. For example, if your Moon is in Capricorn then you have come from the Capricorn tribe, or alternatively, you have previously graduated from the University of Capricorn.

This is who you used to be and what you came into the life with, including a set of specific habits, attitudes, addictions, expectations, skill sets, impressions, and instincts of the gods and goddesses, or archetypes, of the past lineage. It also contributes information as to your way of life, relationship style and previous set of intentions.

Importantly, in Shamanic Astrology, the Moon placement is not a female, or goddess symbol. It includes gods and goddesses and is not restricted to a culturally understood gender. The Moon is like a depository of the previous experiences, attitudes and instinctual impressions. Knowledge about your Moon, that is to say "lineage," can be tremendously useful for understanding your attitudes or expectations. (Read the sections about the Gods, Goddesses and the archetypes of the sign of your Moon.)

Most importantly, this knowledge of your lineage provides a marvelous framework or template from which to have compassion for your own predicaments – and we all have them.

SECOND MOVEMENT

In Shamanic Astrology, the second movement is sometimes called the tools and equipment for the current life intent. For the purposes of this book, we shall primarily focus on the archetypes for the gods and goddess. These will be the all important natal sign placements of Venus and Mars. This is the essential material in order to "be your archetype." This material is further elucidated in Chapter Ten: "The Cards – The Gods and the Goddesses."

Mars for Men

Mars, by sign, represents the version of masculinity, the specific expression of the archetype of the god, that a man is born to develop familiarity with and ultimately mastery of, in this lifetime. Whether understood as stemming from intentional choice prior to birth or simply a manifestation of natural law, the symbol is an extremely important and potent foundational statement of a man's original intent.

Venus for Women

Venus, by sign, represents the version of femininity, the specific expression of the archetype of the goddess that a woman was born to develop familiarity with and ultimately mastery of, in this lifetime. Whether understood as stemming from intentional choice prior to birth or simply a manifestation of natural law, the symbol is an extremely important and potent foundational statement of a woman's original intent.

At this point, if you are wondering about the Sun sign consider this: about two out of every five women have the Sun and Venus in the same sign and only one out of every twelve men have Mars and the Sun in the same sign. It is only when a woman has Venus and the Sun in the same sign and when a Man has Mars and the Sun in the same sign that some of the general, mainstream Sun sign descriptions will appear to apply. However, this will always be relative to the current cultural interpretation of that sign. The Venus and Mars placements are what determine the current life intent of femininity and masculinity through the archetype itself, while the Sun sign simply indicates where one is born according to the seasonal calendar. When Venus (for women) or Mars (for men) are the same as the Sun sign, then the archetype, goddess or god, is burning its own fuel. There is an energetic and seasonal match, and no ambiguity whatsoever, as to what goddess or god one is.

Mars for Women

Mars, on a woman's chart, represents the archetype of masculinity she resonates with and responds to. Initially, and usually, this god image is seen as the projected "other." In the psychological and spiritual process of the "Sacred Marriage" this external image of the male that a woman responds to can be internally integrated, creating wholeness. Then Mars becomes the symbol of the inner other or inner beloved. For many reasons, it's essential on so many levels for a woman to be familiar with the version of masculinity symbolized by her Mars archetype. These archetypal images work across biological lines. For example, two women in a same sex relationship will nevertheless project and then respond to their Mars archetype.

Venus for a Man

Venus, on a man's chart, represents the archetype of femininity he resonates with and responds to. Initially, and usually, this goddess image is seen as the projected "other." In the psychological and spiritual process of the "Sacred Marriage" discussed later in this book, this external image of the female that a man responds to can be internally integrated, creating wholeness. Then Venus becomes the symbol of the inner other or inner beloved. For many reasons, it's essential on so many levels for a man to be familiar with the version of femininity symbolized by his Venus archetype. Note, these archetypal images work across biological lines. For example, two men in a same sex relationship will nevertheless project and then respond to their Venus archetype.[5]

THREE DEFINITIONS

Projection a completely natural process whereby an unconscious characteristic of one's own is perceived in another person (or any other object or symbol).

Anima from "soul" Latin, the unconscious, feminine side of a man's personality. She is personified often in dreams and through the projection by the full spectrum of images and archetypes of the twelve feminine Venus placements for a man.

Animus from "spirit" Latin, the unconscious, masculine side of a woman's personality. He is personified often in dreams and through the projection by the full spectrum of images and archetypes of the twelve masculine Mars placements for a woman.

THE THIRD MOVEMENT

The Third Movement of the journey of the soul is the storyline of current life purpose. The main symbols for the Third Movement in Shamanic Astrology are the angles of the chart. The Ascendant symbolizes a personal identity project, the self. The Descendent is the partnership and relationship project, the other or others. The Mid-heaven, or MC, is the right livelihood project. The bottom of the chart, the IC, is the home and roots project. It is necessary to have a somewhat exact birth time to have this information available because the signs of the angles change about every two hours and this information will truly individualize the chart by clearly defining the life intent.

The combination of the Ascendant and Descendent is also called the Axis of Partnership and Relationship (see Appendices). In general, this part of the script, the Third Movement, describes the destinations and objectives of the gods or goddesses and offers major clues as to the actual dharma (duty) and way of life that the individual gods and goddesses have intended to explore. The Ascendant can be said to be the directional flow of the soul. All four angles are important for a comprehensive understanding of life purpose. However, this book will emphasize only the Ascendant/ Descendant axis. The twelve signs of the Ascendant, therefore, are rather like the twelve tribes of the Moon, but now as twelve schools of inquiry, often called the mystery schools, for current life purpose.

In summary, in the journey of the soul, we come into the life from the Moon position, the lineage, with the instincts and impressions of the gods and goddesses of the Moon. We choose the time and season to be born, the Sun sign, with a specific expression of the goddess or god – twenty four of them: twelve sign placements for Mars and twelve sign placements for Venus. We investigate the Rising sign, or the Ascendant, with the specific intention of exploring a new school or a new tribe, with a new way of relating and being in partnership, represented by the Descendant, in other words – the Ascendant/Descendant axis. If our Moon and Ascendant are in the same sign, it indicates we are not first time explorers of that school.

To maximize the use of this book, you will need to know the following things: your Moon sign, your Venus and Mars signs, your Rising sign – the Ascendant, and its opposite – the Descendant. To know all these requires a somewhat exact birth time, usually within about thirty minutes. However, if you only know your Venus and Mars, the information about the twenty-four gods and goddesses will be remarkably useful and hopefully, liberating. All this information can be found online or by contacting a Shamanic Astrologer.

A SPECIAL NOTE ABOUT INTENT

Intent is sometimes synonymous with purpose. The word intent comes from the Latin *intendere*, meaning to turn one's attention, to stretch out or to extend or sometimes to lean towards. It is not, in my view, the same as purpose, rather, it is the design for purpose and is actional, including a sense of will and volitional thought. Interestingly, the word "intense" was originally the past participle of intendere, meaning to stretch out. However, "intense" diverged from intent some time later. I rather like the sense of the word intent, meaning an actual will that intends to align with a purpose, that is to say, its own nature. Therefore, "original intent" is completely equivalent to Jung's statement that "free will is to gladly do what we must do." A person can consciously choose, as an actional volition, to align with their own nature, or not. It seems, that with the possible exception of cetaceans and maybe cephalopods, human beings have the greatest freedom to not be their own true nature. Hence, the need to gain distance from the overlays of cultural conditioning and consensus reality and to inquire into our actual archetypal nature. That is the project of this book.

A POSSIBLE MYTHIC SCENARIO
OF THE JOURNEY OF THE SOUL

While no claim is being made as to the literalness of the three movements, or even the necessity for literalness, I offer a possible and workable storyline. Remember here, that the importance of the mythic framework is that it works and assists in providing meaning of a practical nature and, who knows, there could also be some literalness. Following death, the soul encounters the proverbial, or metaphoric, "lords of karma," which can also be called the "reviewing board." The Buddhist view is that this experience is a projection of our own mind, as a life review takes place. I prefer this view, rather than to project onto an externalized authority.

Then, the time comes to choose the next life. All factors can be taken into account, including family history, DNA, and the non-Christianized karma described earlier. The Moon position on the chart would represent these factors. Suppose, for example, the Moon is in Libra, indicating that lifetimes of experiences of culturally appropriate relational experiences are in this person's repertoire; lives well lived as wife or husband, according to the moirés of the time period in history, almost always a pair bonder for life; lifetimes of representing the foundational values that hold the generations together through relational commitment. This can include everything from arranged marriages, to actually being with a soul-mate, or twin flame. In all cases, the core identity would always be based on the "other," or "others." Actions would not be taken without first checking it out through the reflection in a partner's eyes or the eyes of other people. Great social skills and generally harmonious and peace-making behavior will have predominated. Included in this "history" would be happiness and suffering, success and failure. But, in summary, this individual would have been highly skilled in Libra behavior, quite the expert, actually. It had all been an investigation of the Libra Mystery School, also known as the Libra tribe.

So, this individual, having completed the review, is at that creative volitional point of "intending" the next life. Based on the foundation of the past experience (the Moon) then: "What to do?" It would certainly be possible to decide to keep the same script, the same storyline. In that case, the incarnation would be with a Libra Venus, for a woman, or a Libra Mars for a man, creating just a minor variation, or a continuation, of the known and familiar skill set.

But, the Libra Moon individual could just as easily be finished with Libra or even bored with Libra. Might it not be fun, exciting, or audacious to try something else? It could even just be curiosity. What if this Libra Moon was curious about Scorpio? Incarnation occurs then with Venus in Scorpio, for a woman, or Mars in Scorpio, for a man. The archetypal characteristics of Scorpio are completely different from Libra. Rather than being culturally appropriate and other oriented, the Scorpio investigation is one of passion and feeling and most importantly the realm of desire. Desire, for Scorpio, is the engine of creation, arising from self-interest. This means the project is to be aware and capable of responding directly to one's own desires and feelings, with no reference to the "other." Rather than the rational, left brained Libran expression with interest in husbands, wives and partner imagery, or harmonious and culturally appropriate behavior, Scorpio takes a right brained, irrational approach which could involve choices that are often considered culturally dangerous by society.

Scorpio is more about going to the edge, and as a friend once said, "You can't see the edge until you are slightly past the edge and look back." Rather than actions tempered by ideas and mental relational feedback, as with Libra, Scorpio either feels it or doesn't. It's wild and unpredictable. Social conventions are irrelevant. Ancient, mythic imagery for Scorpio would include the sorceress witch, the wild man in the woods, explorers of the Underworld: Pele, Hecate, Pan, etc. This will be elaborated upon further in Chapter Twelve, The Cards: The Twelve Mystery Schools.

If Venus or Mars is in Scorpio, the intent is to experience the space of that archetype, and then to learn how to master it. This is exactly why it's so important to know what sign your Venus and Mars are in, particularly, if these positions are substantially different from the Moon archetype. In this case, it is critical to address the archetypes of Venus or Mars. Many people can remain over-identified, as if addicted, to their Moon position.

Another thing to always remember about this is that a good number of the Venus and Mars placements are either not well-known or are much criticized and made wrong in some way. In this system, there are no good or bad placements. All are authentic and legitimate expressions of the goddesses and gods of femininity and masculinity.

Now, going back to our example, Scorpio is vastly different from Libra. It HAS been heavily judged against. It would be very understandable that this person, in discovering the challenges of Scorpio and the heavy judgments against it, could hide it away, in fear of being dangerous to oneself and/ or others. In some cases, the other extreme is found, that of rash and reckless behavior. Both examples stem from the same cause. These individuals are beginners with Scorpio and experts with Libra. This lifetime the focus is on the investigation of Scorpio and it is clearly the intent to investigate and then master Scorpio, sooner or later. It would be easy to imagine, in this example, the person at some point wondering, "What was I thinking in choosing to explore Scorpio after being such a good Libra?" But the choice has been made. The way that it seems to work is that once birth has occurred, it's not possible to inform that metaphorical reviewing board that you have changed your mind!

Summarizing this example, so far: the Moon, in this case, in Libra, is the ancient and established identity. This individual is not even initially aware of the new set of instructions. The Libra Moon instinctually desires to uphold and preserve what it's previously known dharma (duty) to be. It's actually a survival thing. The former Libran does not want to let go of the previously established identity. Then incarnation happens with a new set of intentions, including a Sun sign indicating the time and season of the new life. Most importantly, the individual enters into this new life with particular Venus and Mars placements which are the most specific set of instructions for current life purpose. The entirety of the life journey is like a workshop for exploring, what will likely be, quite a contrast from what was previously known.

In the long run, it's not about being completely, 100 percent, the Mars or Venus archetypes and never expressing the Moon. Rather, a useful and harmonious formula would be to embody and express the Venus or Mars archetype two thirds of the time and the Moon archetype, one third, but never embodying and expressing the Moon position over 50 percent of the time. So, in this example, Mars or Venus in Scorpio, or Scorpio Rising, will ultimately be more important than the Libra Moon, whilst resting on a healthy foundation of the Libra Moon. This person will never completely be of self-interest and only motivated by spontaneous passion, feeling and desire. There will remain a certain objective and mental sensitivity to others and to relational and other social conventions.

FOR THOSE WHO KNOW THEIR BIRTH TIME

This example is not complete without mentioning the Ascendant (Rising Sign) and Descendant. This part of the story can only be discerned from a somewhat exact birth time. Do note, that even without this information, just knowing the Venus and Mars archetypes can be unbelievably useful. But, if you do know your time of birth, here is how it works.

The twelve rising signs are likened to twelve theatres of life. It's as if central casting, or a great director, has assigned you a role as a god or goddess (your Venus or Mars archetype) and then instructs you to perform that role in one of these twelve theatres. The fact that these theatres of life change about every two hours is why the birth time is needed. For this understanding of the life process, you, yourself, are that director. In this Libra/Scorpio example, the rising sign will provide an additional set of instructions relating to the dharma (duty) of the current life intent. Please refer to the detailed descriptions of the categories of the life process in the next chapter. The Scorpio god or goddess will develop differently, depending on whether the theatre of life is, for example, a householder/culture bearer path rather than a free electron path, or whether the theatre is in service to spirit or more of self-interest, etc.

the Ascendant

the rising sign

the personal enlightenment path

CHAPTER SIX

The Categories of the Life Process

In order to utilize the Shamanic Astrology Divination Card Deck most effectively, these categories of the astrological mysteries will help elucidate a greater understanding of the twenty-four gods and goddesses and Mystery Schools. The twelve signs or mystery schools are first divided into three categories also known as the quadruplicities. These categories describe three different ways of life/dharmas.[2]

HOUSEHOLDER or CULTURE BEARER

Aries, Cancer, Libra, Capricorn. This way of life prioritizes the maintenance and continuity of civilization and culture over time. Whilst not always literally meaning having a house with children, these four archetypal and astrological mystery schools, are the ones that hold the culture together from one generation to the next. This is related to the Native American injunction: "Make no decisions save for the benefit of the seven generations to follow." The four schools included here are usually called the Cardinal Signs and the Cardinal Quadruplicity by mainstream astrology. The Householder/ Culture Bearer dharmas are "in the world" and are generally "other oriented." Globally and historically, these describe four well-known archetypal roles. They are generally the most secular, meaning living in the world, or worldly, and not belonging to a religious order, from late Latin "saecularis" meaning worldly.

> **Cancer:** Water, feeling function, mother, nurturer, family, clan, the giver of social and cultural love.

Capricorn: Earth, sensation function, father, teacher, family, clan, the circle of grandmothers, the giver of responsibility, social and cultural structure.

Libra: Air, thinking function, partner, husband, wife, friend, social and cultural beliefs.

Aries: Fire, intuition function, protector, warrior, hunter, provider, social and cultural protection.

SERVICE TO SPIRIT

Gemini, Virgo, Sagittarius, Pisces: These four are called the Mutable Signs or the Mutable Quadruplicity by mainstream astrology. With the dharma of Service to Spirit, the priorities of life are directed to transcendent, transpersonal and/or spiritual and impersonal pursuits not directly related to the secular or householder realms. There is no connection, at all, to the self-interest category. Unlike the other orientedness of the householder group, these four are spirit oriented. By spirit, I'm using the connotation of that word suggested by David Abram in his remarkable book, *The Spell of the Sensuous*, in which spirit means "that which is not human." This includes animals, nature, and the entire realm of sensory and perceptual experience, not related to secular, worldly human endeavors. And more recently (the last three thousand years), not related to or determined by the abstract creations of the human mind starting first with the alphabet and now through the vast extension of the cybernetic World Wide Web. These four mystery schools include the following archetypal roles:

Gemini: Air, thinking function, impersonal and transpersonal, actor, holy fool, Puer/Puella (eternal youth), magician, psycho-pomp (guide for souls), heyokah, free of secular or personal entanglements and in service to spirit through complete surrender to the non-dual, irrational dictates of spirit.

Virgo: Earth, sensation function, impersonal, priest/priestess, ceremonialist in service to the ecology of the web of life and worship of Great Mystery.

Sagittarius: Fire, intuition function, seeker, explorer, adventurer free of secular or worldly attachments, impersonal and transpersonal, in service to the Truth through taking responsibility for one's own liberation first as the best way to be in service to spirit.

Pisces: Water, feeling function, mystic, healer, transpersonally in service to the relief of suffering and the promotion of the liberation and fulfillment of the entire web of life (all sentient beings).

SELF-INTEREST

Taurus, Leo, Scorpio, Aquarius: The four mystery schools of self-interest prioritize the direct experience of the individual through the four modalities or elements of life. These are never other oriented or in service to spirit or concerned much with the secular. Self-interest is not taken to mean "selfish" or anything pejorative. The willful intention towards one's self-interest and own experience is the authentic and necessary raison d'être and the primary purpose of these signs. They are known as the four Fixed Signs, or Fixed Quadruplicity, in mainstream astrology. These four, historically and globally, portray these archetypal roles:

Taurus: Earth, sensation function, lover, epicure, sensualist, intimacy and art as ends in themselves. Enjoying simply being through a receptive or receiving modality. Beauty and aesthetics and intimacy as art are the contributions.

Scorpio: Water, feeling function, sorcerer, witch, shaman, wild man in the woods, Pan. Intimacy and art as ends in themselves through an active, direct modality. The strongest will and deepest urge to go past the edges of possible personal experience via the feelings is the contribution.

Leo: Fire, intuition function, King/Queen, leader, creator, the strongest will to create for its own sake. The experience of the self for its own sake and to innocently experience the creative place on the wheel of life is its greatest contribution.

Aquarius: Air, thinking function, intellectual, scientist, innovator, visionary. The strongest will to take the mind and consciousness as far as possible for its own sake. To courageously extend and expand the mind; and to freely expand beyond the known boundaries are its greatest contributions.

Note, these descriptions of the three dharma categories and the three quadruplicities of the twelve mystery schools, has purposely not included negative or "shadow" expressions or roles.

Several other categories now require some explanation.

GIVERS/RECEIVERS

The Givers: Cancer, Capricorn, Virgo, Pisces
An additional motivation and purpose of these four is in the modality called "Giving." Not only are they not of self-interest, but in order to fulfill their function some external object must exist that needs their knowledge, nourishment, or other skill set from which to receive.

Cancer, as a Householder/Culture bearer dharma, gives and provides personal and hierarchical nourishment and love to children, clients, students, employees, pets, plants, etc.

Capricorn, as a Householder/Culture bearer dharma, gives mostly impersonal, hierarchical knowledge and structure to children, clients, students, employees, *chelas*, etc. These always involve some version of hierarchical giving. These are authentic, hierarchical relationships and they are completely motivated by the desire to give but will need receivers, or those who genuinely need and desire to be given to.

Virgo, as an in Service to Spirit dharma, gives and provides selfless service, impersonally honoring and worshipping the sacred fabric and web of life in life-long, ceremonial dedication to the earth and sky and her divine patterning.

Pisces, as an in Service to Spirit dharma, transpersonally gives and provides healing and loving compassion to wherever sorrow, suffering and grief are felt in the Universe, without any personal distinctions, or preferences. There is an unconditional commitment to serve all life to fulfill its journey to liberation.

None of the giver dharmas are concerned with self and all are motivated by the awareness of some need (nurture, teaching, ceremony, healing, etc.) which they then have the required function to provide.

The Receivers: Taurus, Leo

There is only one mystery school that is a complete receiver and that is Taurus. Taurus holds the secrets to true and authentic receivership. Again, this has nothing to do with selfishness or anything pejorative. Taurus gives value to the givers. There can be nothing more enjoyable for a giver than to be with a good receiver and the skills of Taurus include knowing what is actually good, not indiscriminate receiving.

The only other one of the twelve that has a bit of the receiving essence is Leo. Leo certainly thrives and is at its healthiest when receiving praise and adoration. While it's certainly a truth that all human beings enjoy receiving praise there is something extra magical that happens for the Leo type receiving praise. The other mystery schools are either pretty neutral on the giving and receiving scale or it's entirely a non-issue.

RELATIONAL CATEGORIES

In order to completely understand the relational attributes of the twenty-four archetypes of the goddess and god there are a few additional categories to introduce and define.

Personal: By this I mean personally relational, one to one, non-hierarchical capacities, with an interest and ability to share the most personal content of one's life. I don't mean data, information, linear history or resumes. These really "personal qualities" are not definable. They cannot be perfected, or even learned by some technique or training. This personalness is what a person means when they say, "I want to be loved for me." It's also what, in the Sufi tradition, is known as the "pearl," or the pearl beyond price. Taurus and Libra are primarily personal.

Transpersonal: Here the previously described "personal qualities" are greatly valued, but are applied to everyone collectively and universally without the interest or ability to choose one specific person. Pisces and Aquarius are primarily transpersonal.

Impersonal: The impersonal mystery schools are either not interested in, or not capable of, being personal or transpersonal in the sense of valuing or honoring the previously described personal qualities and content. Virgo, Capricorn, Gemini and Sagittarius are all primarily impersonal.

Hierarchical: These mystery schools are authentically hierarchical, meaning that there is some kind of ranking with an intended distancing in order to perform their function. Examples include parents to children, teachers to students, gurus to *chelas* and therapists to clients. Cancer and Capricorn are primarily hierarchical. Virgo and Pisces can be to a degree.

Pair Bonding: There are many people today, and some cultures historically, that have believed that all human beings are, by nature, pair bonders. By pair bonding I mean finding one person to mate or "bond" with, generally understood to be for life. This belief system believes this bonding essence is true for everyone. Pair-bonding has also included the concept of monogamy. They aren't really the same, as we'll be seeing. The view of this work is that pair bonding is a completely natural and authentic intention of some people, but certainly not all, not even most. The pair bond intention and dharma almost always is found with the Libra and Aries Mystery Schools and some of the time with Capricorn and Cancer, particularly when there are the commitments associated with raising a family. There can be found a clear distinction between the archetypal essence of the authenticity of the pair bond as a relational choice, as with Libra and Aries, and a pair bond choice arising from Cancer and Capricorn that is much more motivated by the practical realities of what it takes to raise a family in a patriarchal culture. The realities were quite a bit different in the matrilineal and matriarchal cultures.

Monogamy: The authentic intention for monogamy, here defined as sexual intimacy with one person, only, at a time, either serially or for life, is also most often found with Libra, Aries, Cancer and Capricorn with much the same cultural and historical logic as previously mentioned.

However, monogamy and pair bonding are not always equivalent. For example, the category of pair bonding can be conceived of as having an extreme left wing and an extreme right wing with lots of variations in between. An extreme left wing would be an extremely all in, completely committed, pair bond couple, who can choose to include sexual intimacy with others, but always within the context of the bond. This expansion of sexual intimacy is always for the purpose of deepening the strength and depth of the primary bond. So this would not be monogamy but is very much a pair bond.

On the extreme right wing would be the totally committed, pair bond couple with a total and inviolate focus on only their intimacy with each other and no deviation or distraction from the full attention only on the chosen partner as the object of desire. This end of the spectrum is without a question completely monogamous and as a choice, not for moral or ethical reasons.

In between these two extremes exists quite a range of possibilities, nearly all being monogamous. For example, some pair bonders welcome and enjoy sexual fantasy and flirtation with others, they see aliveness and magic in it, while others naturally have no interest in this and would even consider such behavior a waste of time. Recent discussions as to whether internet sex is cheating, or not, would fall somewhere into this discussion. From the perspective of the pair bonder, the bottom line would be to determine if the internet sex or other forms of fantasy deepened the intimacy of the pair bond. That would be its purpose with reference to monogamy.

In summary, pair bonding and/or monogamy can be authentic choices that are an expression of the original intent of certain archetypes: Libra and Aries, mainly, and Cancer and Capricorn, often.

But this is not true of others. It's somewhat like the question asked about whether human beings are vegetarian, carnivores, or omnivores. Looking at the length of the stomach and the digestive tract, or the nature of the teeth, there is no clear answer to this question. Even taking into account culture and geography it's still a choice: not all people are the same. Fortunately, this knowledge of the archetypes provides some amazing clues as to what would be most empowering to choose.

Polyamory: This relational dharma means the ability and desire to be personally intimate, including sexually, with more than one person at a time without any reference to a pair bond. This path is not the same as promiscuity or recreational sexuality, which can be understood as sexuality without personal intimacy. The polyamorous dharma can be with one or many. It is deeply, personally intimate and includes sexual relationships, all with their own individual agreements and commitments, but never with the expectation or desire for the all in, exclusive, defined pair bond. The polyamorous dharma can experience a depth of personal intimacy equal to the depth of the pair bond dharma. Certain ancient cultures had great respect for this way of life, often described as the way of the courtesan. The mystery schools of polyamory are mainly Scorpio and Taurus and sometimes Leo.

The Free Electron: Considerably different from the pair bonders and the polyamorous are the free electrons. The natural and authentic intention is for freedom and autonomy. Deep personal intimacy is not a high priority and the concept of pair bonding is perceived of as bondage. There exists here a natural desire for spaciousness and unencumbered non-attachment. Personal intimacy and sexuality can be recreational, adventurous, experimental or, in some cases, can remain rather low on the list of priorities. This isn't a deficiency of personal intimacy qualities, rather, the greater interest and attention is elsewhere. Gemini, Sagittarius, Aquarius and sometimes Leo are the main mystery schools of the free electron.

The Renunciate: These are non-secular, non-relational, and non-personal dharmas. In other time periods in history a greater percentage of the population had this dharma or were required to fit into it. The current era of history is not the only one that has limited the full expression and spectrum of masculinity and femininity. For example, in the Middle Ages and the Dark Ages, if a woman was deemed unfit, uninterested or unsuccessful at marriage, she could always go to a convent. It was often the only other acceptable path for a woman. Otherwise, there were the stigmatized paths of witches or prostitutes. Much of great value has been written of this elsewhere. But in the current age, most everyone, pretty much all the archetypes, are on some kind of a relational path. All the gods and goddesses are learning more about themselves through personal relational experience in the world. So, there are far fewer people who are authentically intending a renunciate dharma. It remains, however, a valid choice for some archetypes. Most often the renunciate dharmas are found in the mystery schools of Virgo, Pisces and Sagittarius.

Sacred Relationship: Without question, this dharma and relational category is the least understood. It's best to start with what it's not. It's not pair bonding, it's not polyamory, it's not recreational, it's not secular and it's not personal. The primary characteristics are that healing can take place and that the relating takes place in sacred space. There is generally a connection with a process of initiation. Extremely often the experiences happen outside of time and/or in secret. This dharma has been hidden and often forbidden and has just recently begun to come out of the shadows. Included in this dharmic category are varieties of sexual healing modalities, some aspects of the world of Tantra, different forms of sexual/spiritual initiation, shamanism, and ecstatic rites of passage as is described in the work of Sylvia Perera, particularly the book: *Celtic Queen Maeve*. Most often this dharma can be found in the Mystery Schools of Virgo, Pisces, and Gemini.

GALACTIC ALIGNMENT

galactic alignment

WILD CARDS

WILD CARDS

maximum renewal
spiritual initiation for the
turning of the ages

Maximum Renewal the Turning
of the Ages!

Gobekli Tepe

CHAPTER SEVEN

A Cosmological Interlude

With the Original Cosmology and Mythos of this Work

The mythological foundation and the worldview of this book (and of Shamanic Astrology) has been primarily inspired and sourced from the pre-Bronze Age civilization of Ireland. These same views have also been found in pre-Aryan Dravidian India and in pre-Zeus dominant, matrilineal Greece. These cosmologies are very consistent throughout the world during the megalithic ages and are features of a time in history known as the Neolithic, or the New Stone Age. The Neolithic times were just before metal working predominated and considerably before the arrival of iron, the metal that solidified the success of the patriarchal domination of the previous ways that human beings organized their world.

A primary feature of the Neolithic times of history was the relatively equal balance between hunter gatherer lifestyles and the early development of some agriculture. A result of this balance was a generally egalitarian culture, with minimal separations of class and hierarchy or the rule by a small elite. Most importantly, for this book, the Neolithic times demonstrated a pretty equal balance and equality between men and women. History texts will offer suggested dates for the Neolithic Age, usually something like 6,000 BCE through 1,500 BCE. But there is great variance in different parts of the world. The Neolithic Age lasted well up to the mid-1400s in North America, for example, and almost that long in Polynesia.

The date of its beginnings keeps being pushed back, recently to possibly 12,000 BC, with the discovery and excavation of the megaliths of Gobekli Tepe, in Southeastern Turkey. Meanwhile, in Ireland the Megalithic/ Neolithic period is roughly 4,000 BC through 1,700 BC Their mythic cosmology certainly originated earlier than this, arriving into Ireland probably from Iberia, Brittany, the Mediterranean (Sardinia and Malta) and North Africa. The original cosmology of the Neolithic and Megalithic Ages still animate the land and spirit of Ireland because of Ireland's geographical remoteness and the very special way in which Celtic Christianity honored the older ways.

Here is a summary of Irish cosmology. The first principle is clearly female, known as *Boand,* or *Boi*, or *Boa*. The power of the gods is confirmed within the limits of the goddess who is seen as the creatrix of the All. It's the goddess who confers that status of godhead upon the *Dagda* (the original male deity), whose position as god is entirely dependent upon his union with her cosmic force. A cosmological order was then established wherein the ceremony of a coronation marriage occurred. The status of sovereignty was bestowed upon the king by the goddess. In these earliest formulations this original creatrix energy became a triple goddess, generally with the following features:

1. Life and abundance.
2. Death and war.
3. Mysticism and prophesy.

An ancient name of Ireland was *Banba*, meaning "the land of the women." Ireland, or Eire, is named after the ancient goddess Eiru. The mythic and legendary race known as the *Thua De Danaan* are believed to be the designers and builders of the massive megalithic ceremonial structures, such as the massive chambered cairn at New Grange, where celebrations took place over thousands of years to demonstrate how the sun, moon and stars could enter deep into the earth, demonstrating a spiritual and practical union of sky and land and between male and female. Thousands of years of peace resulted. The name, *Thua De Danaan*, actually means "the people of the goddess." Their name was connected to the goddesses Danu or Anu, and they were clearly matrilineal.

The Medieval tales of King Arthur, Avalon, Merlin and the Knights of the Round Table represented a cyclical and perpetual revival of the deep longing of post patriarchal peoples in a world where the masculine and feminine lived, loved and worked together as equals and allies. The King Arthur mythos was originally inspired by the Irish *Thua De Danaan* and their times, when the mythic reality of Camelot and Avalon actually existed. The longing for balance and the resonant polarity of masculine and feminine has remained alive and will continue to resurface, over and over again, until the excesses of either dominator patriarchy or female superior matriarchy disappear: the "once and future king," indeed.

In India, particularly in the southern Indian Dravidian culture, Shakti, the feminine power, is the active universal principle for which Shiva, the masculine, is receptive and supplicant to. Of course, the god, Shiva, whilst recognizing that the power and the active force is with Shakti, can, in fact, rise up to meet her in equal union. Shakti means cosmic energy, power, ability, capacity, strength, prowess, "the power inherent in a cause to produce its necessary effect," and also represents the female genitalia. Shakti is the active power of a deity and is regarded, spiritually and mythologically, as the goddess/consort and queen. The Tantra Sutras say, "The female principle antedates and includes the male principle" and "this female principle is the supreme divinity."

In Ancient Greece, the Archai, the first principles, or starting points, were frequently seen as:

1. Ananke, meaning necessity.
2. Nous, meaning reason.

Ananke is feminine, whilst Nous, with its connection to consciousness and time is a masculine word. Nous always was somehow subservient to Ananke and could not rule or contain her. Here then are three examples of cosmological first principles and starting points that all begin with the feminine and offer clues as to how the masculine can be an equal principle. This discussion leads directly into the extremely thorny issue of the masculine and feminine itself when applied to men and women and gods and archetypes.

In the lyrics from the song entitled, "Essence" by The Church, writer Steve Kilby explains the situation beautifully:

The universe is female
Eluding the science of men
You sway and you swagger and your neat/mean little dagger
You're going to blow it again

Prove her existence in everything
The soul of her rivers and stones
Her acquiescence to everything
Her essence, her presence, her bones

Lust and law take the masculine
Ambition and war take the boy
I pin the tail on the alpha male
A little man making big noise

It's not the engine or chassis
It's not the weapon or length
Your war dance I guess got this place in a mess
But there's something that's stronger than strength

A metaphor is a goddess
A king that's fit for a queen
The opposite side of that armored old hide
I hope you know what I mean
Oh yeah[8]

Countless examples exist in the current age demonstrating tremendous confusion about sexuality and gender. There seems to be no consistent agreement or consensus about what men or women are supposed to be. What are the definitions of masculinity and femininity?

In order to reach an accurate and useful mapping system, or typology, it's important to recognize, and then see through, the cultural and historical overlays onto these core concepts.

This is no easy task. As a starting point, the approach of this book makes a clear distinction between the physical, biological reality of a man and woman and whatever masculinity and femininity actually are archetypally. Men, as biological organisms, can be defined as having XY chromosomes with male genitals, or a lingam, using the more elegant, non-English word. Women are XX chromosome beings with female genitalia, including the yoni. That part is clear. (We are leaving out of this discussion the complex issues dealing with hermaphrodism, etc.) But how does that translate into masculinity and femininity? The word "gender," for example, does not help much because until recently gender simply meant the usual and conventionally ascribed characteristics of how masculinity and femininity are believed to be, as defined by a specific culture and in a specific time period in history.

In pondering these issues I read an amazing article by Rene Malamud in the book, *Facing the Gods*, edited by James Hillman.[9] The discussion involved gender descriptions and assumptions about masculine and feminine as being projections. I came upon the following quote: "The projection does not lie where a first glance indicates it to be, i.e., in biological or sociological conditions, but in the psychic polarity between Luna and Sol." EXACTLY!

The projection exists even beyond the recognition of the recent historical impact of the patriarchal expressions of male/female roles, and seeing those as the projections that they are. Beyond the obvious physical differences between men and women is found this unexamined and often unquestionably accepted major projection. Most people I have known assume that the Sun is masculine and the Moon is feminine. Isn't this assumption obvious? Well, actually, not really. The further one goes back into history, the more often the discovery is made of the many Moon gods and the many Sun goddesses. Even now, in the German and Japanese languages, the word for Sun is feminine and there is a masculine word for the Moon.

Although this is not an exhaustive list, the following languages have a masculine Moon and a feminine Sun: Norwegian, Lithuanian, German–Teutonic, Sanskrit, Swedish, ancient Anglo-Saxon, Sumerian, Arabic, Egyptian, Japanese, and many from South America. The Norse word, *Sunna*, is the Sun goddess and the Anglo-Saxon word, *Mona*, is a masculine word for the Moon god. Those words are, of course, the originals for the English, Sun and Moon. Meanwhile, Latin, French, Greek, Italian, Portuguese and generally all the Romance languages have it the "usual" way. In Egypt, the goddess *Sekhmet* is the Sun goddess and *Thoth* is the Moon god. In mythic Ireland, *Grainne* (also *Graian* or *Graine*) was the Sun goddess.

Brighid, or *Brigid* (there are so many spellings of her name) was also a solar goddess. *Diarmuid* may be a Moon god. There are also many Sun gods in Ireland, for example, *Lugh*, and lots of Moon goddesses. In contemporary Irish Gaelic, however, the word for the Moon is a feminine word, *Gealach*, while the Sun is the old feminine word, *Grian*. Fittingly, in the land of the Goddess, both Sun and Moon are feminine!

I can share a personal experience that shattered my own unconscious, projected beliefs. I've always loved and been drawn to the great stone circles of Northwest Scotland, particularly the Callanish complex on the island of Lewis, in the Outer Hebrides.

One year, I was facilitating a small group at Callanish. Over a number of previous times we became aware that a triangular arrangement of stones inside the stone circle known as Callanish III, exactly matched the patterns of the three stars known by astronomers as the Summer Triangle. These stars are Vega, Altair and Deneb. Three very different and distinct stones exactly mirrored, in their spacing within the circle, the spacing of these three stars in the sky; a perfect, "as above, so below" expression. We had, furthermore, learned that the shapes and colors of the stones corresponded to the ancient, Neolithic conceptions of the Triple Goddess. One stone was clearly the Maiden, one clearly the Mother and one represented the Crone.

However, there was a fourth stone in the circle set apart from the three goddess stones. With my astronomical background, I could see this fourth stone was along the line of the ecliptic, the path the Sun, Moon and planets are on, relative to the other three stars/stones. For years, on previous trips, I and other members of the group tried unsuccessfully to decipher the mystery of this fourth stone. If you look at the picture, it's obviously a male stone. We called it the Green Man or the Green God. But was it Mars? Was it possibly Jupiter? Or even the Sun? Nothing seemed quite right.

Then, in a flash, the projected assumptions suddenly faded away and it was at once obvious that it was the Moon, a crescent Moon.

And sure enough there are Moon gods who show up as crescent Moons in Neolithic times. Horneblend, an agate attributed to the Moon and found in other special stones connected with the Moon in other circles was also greatly in evidence in this particular stone.

Megalithic stones at Callanish

A final certainty of this awakening to the presence of the Moon god is that the Callanish stone circle complex is oriented to a range of mountains resembling a reclining woman, known as the *Cailleach na Mointeach* or "The Old Woman of the Moors." Every nineteenth year, when the extreme southern declination Moon rises and sets low and parallel to the horizon, every phase of the Moon, over the course of 18 months, will enter into the body of this woman on the land.

The main point of this discussion isn't to suggest that the current culture has it all backwards and to simply reverse the system. Instead, we propose that the projection of symbolism onto the Sun and the Moon cosmologies include gods AND goddesses. In fact, in our earliest cosmologies, as shown in the three examples given above of Irish, pre-patriarchal Greek and Indian Dravidian culture, there are many gods and goddesses of the Sun and the Moon. This elucidates the major thesis of this book, that there exists throughout history, a tremendous diversity of the authentic expressions of the gods and goddesses. These archetypal symbols can be freed from historical and cultural projections, even the hidden mythic projections onto the Sun and the Moon. (Incidentally, mainstream astrology, as well as the majority of the Pagan Wiccan traditions, have bought into this hidden mythic projection, hook, line and sinker.)

But, is there something still deeper and essentially archetypal about masculinity and femininity beyond biology, behind all projections? I think there is. To be clear, however, I am not proposing androgyny here. This is not an approach desiring the uniting of the characteristics of both sexes. The word androgyny was originally connected to hermaphrodism, and has meant being genderless, or possessing a combination of the female and male traits, whatever those traits may culturally be seen as.

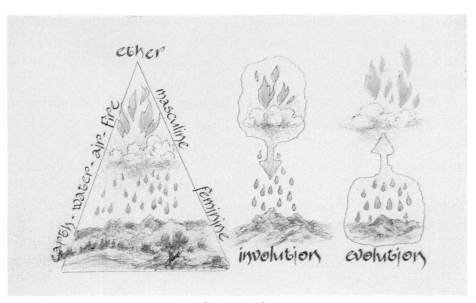

Involution, Evolution

CHAPTER EIGHT

The Four Elements and The New Paradigm

I am proposing here a new foundation for considering the archetypal nature of masculinity and femininity. For this new foundation I will utilize two previously noted concepts:

1. The four elements.
2. Evolution and involution.

Shamanic Astrology accepts the ancient and traditional view that fire and air are archetypally masculine and that earth and water are archetypally feminine. The four elements can also be seen as a gradient from the greatest subtlety to the deepest density: fire to air, air to water and water to earth. The progression begins with fire as pure consciousness and creative intuition. Air, as the thinking function, requires a mind and space, but hardly needs a body. Water as feeling and awareness of human values requires a body and soul. Finally the descent proceeds all the way down and into the densest earth, the deepest involution of spirit into matter.

The life process consists of two complementary journeys. One direction is from density and manifestation, (earth and water), toward mind, consciousness and objectivity, (fire and air). This is called the *Journey of Evolution* from matter and feeling, requiring substance, to mind and spirit, without the need of material substance. Earth and water to air and fire is evolution. The evolutionary path is the MASCULINE journey. It starts in matter, density and sensation and goes up and out to explore mind and consciousness.

The other journey begins in consciousness, mind or spirit and then descends and enters into matter, sensation and density. This is the *Journey of Involution*. Fire and air into earth and water is involution. This second journey, the path of involution, is the FEMININE journey, starting in spirit and intending to go down and into earth and water.

These are completely complementary and equally authentic journeys and not, in any way, based on biology. A man can be on an archetypally feminine *Journey of Involution*: for example, a man with Mars or the Ascendant in an earth or a water sign. Conversely, a woman can be on an archetypally masculine *Journey of Evolution*: women with Venus or the Ascendant in a fire or an air sign are generally on masculine evolutionary journey. (See diagram "Involution, Evolution" on preceding page.)

The intention in sharing this alternative foundation for understanding what actually is the archetypal essence of masculinity and femininity is to solidify the main view of this book – that the full spectrum of the archetypes of the gods and goddesses, in their authenticity and uniqueness, is considerably more important than projected cultural and historical notions of gender and the supposed nature of men and women.

One mythic example, which clearly illustrates the reciprocity of the journeys of evolution and involution is the quite well-known story of the quest for the holy grail. Many different interpretations and versions of this mysterious spiritual quest exist throughout history. The story shows up as part of the previously mentioned Arthurian saga, as well. Here is a version that fits this proposed foundational thesis regarding masculinity and femininity.

A young, idealistic and spiritually oriented knight (male) leaves his land, his home, his brothers, his woman, seeking and searching on a seemingly impossible quest for the grail. There are hundreds of different symbols of the grail. Usually, it's some kind of cup, chalice or bowl, almost always filled with blood or sacramental wine. To find the grail would unquestionably result in attaining something longed for, such as mystical union, enlightenment or wholeness. As I perceive it, what the knight finds is a vessel or receptacle filled with blood, the symbolic imagery of the sacred feminine and essential women's mysteries, much pre-dating Christian overlays. Interestingly, the male travels, on this impossible quest for mystical enlightenment, as far away as possible from his home, family and the females, only to arrive back "home" in service to the sacred feminine in her transpersonal and universal reality.

The four elements have been part of the astrological tradition for thousands of years. This doctrine is one of the oldest in the world. Ancient Buddhist, Greek and Babylonian cultures all used this system and it was incorporated into the astrology of all three cultures. It was used to describe the essential parts and principles of which anything consists or of which the foundational powers of anything are based.

There are a variety of different views about the four elements and how they connect with astrology. I have been inspired and influenced by Dane Rudhyar's linking of astrological and Jungian concepts regarding the four elements. Jung himself had studied and integrated many elements of astrology and alchemy which animated his own theories regarding the four elements. Jung's understanding of the connection between the four elements and the four psychological types has also been a huge influence on my thinking.

The following is the meaning and application of the four elements for this book:

> **Fire:** Function of intuition, right brain, masculine, the sheer intensity of perception, irrational function, actional force; thoughts and preferences that come to mind without reflection.

> **Air:** Function of thinking, left brain, masculine, analytical, rational, consciousness; thinking involving balancing, measuring, reflecting, evaluating, and objectivity.

> **Water:** Function of feeling, right brain, feminine; spontaneously and irrationally determining the value of life and its experience through the arising of the aliveness of feeling for oneself or for others, including empathy but not mind or consciousness based.

Note – feeling is not the same as emotion. Feeling is one of the essential states of experience. Emotion can occur in any element as a reaction to an experience.

Earth: Function of sensation, left brain, feminine, rational; based on kinesthetic, organic, physical sensing and the organization of the life experience ranging from survival to the intensity of physical pleasure. It can use the mind but action is determined by the sensations of the physical embodiment.

Crop circle found in Fox Hill, near Liddington, Wiltshire, England in 2015
Photo by Steven Alexander

CHAPTER NINE

The Inner Sacred Marriage Process

Before taking a detailed look at the full spectrum of the masculine and the feminine by way of the Shamanic Astrology Divination Card Deck (Chapter Ten), one more topic needs to be developed. This is called the *inner sacred marriage process*. This is a further development of what was touched on in Chapter Five with regards to a man's Venus and a woman's Mars placements, which have been termed the Opposite Gender Planet (OGP). Some topics introduced there will be expanded on in this chapter.

To reiterate, a central theme of the Shamanic Astrology Paradigm is in de-emphasizing the Sun sign. Rather, the use of Venus and Mars are found to be more valuable and revealing. This is particularly true when the emphasis is on *intent*, or when seen as a set of instructions.

When using the 24 cards, 12 for Venus and 12 for Mars, this chapter will explain how to use all 24 whether you are male or female. This approach offers remarkable clues about how to work on, and then eventually accomplish the goal of developing wholeness, the aim of the inner sacred marriage process.

These 24 images and descriptions can be used in two ways:

Mars for men, Venus for women (the SPG: same gender planet)

In this case, which is the obvious and straightforward one, these symbols and images represent the intended version of the masculine for men and the feminine for women. In other words, these images may not be how you actually are initially, but what you are intending to develop throughout your life. For many, it's not the path of least resistance. That, often, is the masculine or feminine image that would be associated with your Moon sign.

These positions, for you, are your set of instructions. Eventually, you can learn to master, or at least be comfortable in being your SGP. This approach values a full spectrum of possibilities for the masculine and feminine, and provides the tools for avoiding and transcending the chains of limitations stemming from historical and cultural consensus reality.

The attempt has been made here to integrate and synthesize many images from around the world, as well as taking into account the value that comes from images and stories of the past. Much of this has come through the artwork of Roy Purcell, who designed the cards. This hopefully inspires an approach that recognizes how these images change throughout history, and that new sets of possibilities are arising today. We are establishing a template that recognizes how the gods and goddesses, called in modern terms the astrological archetypes of Venus and Mars, are changing and evolving now.

Once again, with strong emphasis, these Venus and Mars archetypal images and descriptions are NOT to be applied to your Sun sign.

Venus for men, Mars for women (the OGP: opposite gender planet)

Using the images and descriptions in this manner requires a somewhat longer explanation. Venus on a man's chart represents his inner and outer experience of the feminine. Mars on a woman's chart represents her inner and outer experience of the masculine. This is termed the OGP (opposite gender planet).

Several topics must be discussed to more fully understand how this works.

> **Projection**: Initially, the OGP is projected onto others. What is this projection phenomena? "Projection" comes from the Latin *proicere*, which means "to throw forth." This word has been used in so many ways throughout the past centuries. The Shamanic Astrology Paradigm uses it in a very specific way.

But first, let's see how it's not being used. It is not being used in a variety of psychologically common usages. For example, projection is not used here as an unconscious self-defense mechanism characterized by a person who defends themselves against their possible awareness of their negative or undesirable qualities, by projecting or attributing them to others. There is no shadow element associated with the way projection is being used here with Venus and Mars (OGP). It's entirely natural, what most all of us do.

Projection, however, can mean attributing one's unconscious qualities to others. But which ones are you ascribing to the other? This leads to an expanded view of Jung's concepts of the anima and animus.

Anima/Animus: Jung used anima for the female part of a man's personality, and animus for the masculine part of a woman's personality. Unfortunately, Jung's view of the masculine and feminine was severely culturally conditioned, and does not reflect the full spectrum approach advocated here. (At least his views were not as rigid as Freud's!) Jung tended to see a man's anima as his desire for *Soul* as if only a woman could take him there. Furthermore, a woman's animus was her quest for *Spirit* and only a man could take her there. Animus translates out as Spirit. Anima translates as Soul. The additional problem was that all women and all men were expected to have a basic culturally determined view of what masculinity and femininity is.

Alternatively, in the view being presented here, the animus can be used virtually the same way as seeing a woman's Mars as her masculine side, and a man's Venus as his feminine side. But, now, we use this expanded view that there are 12 versions of the anima and 12 versions of the animus.

Jung also conceived of the anima and animus as being unconscious, and that an aim of therapy, or as a part of the process of individuation, was the bringing of the anima or animus to objective awareness or full consciousness. This process was not, however, the entirety of wholeness or all there was to the process of individuation.

NOTE ON INDIVIDUATION

Jung conceived of achieving self-actualization through a process of integrating the conscious and the unconscious. His idea of individuation is a process of transformation whereby the personal and the collective unconscious are brought into consciousness by a variety of methods. He often used dream-work, sand-play, and active imagination. Here we add yet another way.

In the more recent history of Western culture, including its effect on the rest of the world, the phenomena of projection has been the primary methodology for the attempt to make the anima or animus (the OGP) conscious. And this happens through the modern approach to relationship that most importantly includes the experience of romantic love.

It is doubtful that prior to the ascent of the phenomena of romantic love did it work this way. Marriage and long term relationships were, more often than not, based on practical things only such as class, caste, economic status, etc. Romantic love or relationship out of free choice, not controlled by family or culture, was rare if it existed at all.

But more recently, around the world, relationships, why they happen and what motivates our choices, involve so many more factors including romantic love. Some people will still choose or be attracted to someone for primarily practical or responsible reasons. For others it's strictly a mental projection where they respond because someone looks like the picture in their mind. And for some others it's entirely visceral – either you feel it or you don't.

This can be quite clearly perceived and understood by the knowledge of the OGP. These images are projected out into the world. It's why we are attracted to certain types. Also, it helps explain and describe what kinds of experiences are happening in our lives to make us more consciously aware of our inner masculine or feminine.

One possible definition of projection is "a mental image perceived as reality." There can be a danger in over literalizing the projected image. On one level there really isn't anyone "out there. "The person that you have projected the image onto may not be that person, in reality, at all. Possibly it's just an illusion designed to get you more in touch with a legitimate and needed part of yourself, which is your inner masculine or feminine.

The OGP can be thought of as your "inner other." A variety of spiritual traditions have recognized this inner other. For example, in Sufism it has been termed "the guest." It's that other part of our self that has been searched for "out there," but was an inner part of ourselves all the time. The Jungian psychologist James Hollis, has referred to this as the quest for the magical other, in his book: *The Eden Express*.

In more recent times, experience of relationship, extending beyond the traditional needs of established cultural conditions, is how a great many are exploring the quest for wholeness and union with our inner other.

Ultimately, whether we are able to manifest easily the external partner of our dreams, or not, the characteristics of our OGP are actually our own and are to be developed for ourselves. This is called the *inner sacred marriage process*. In the Shamanic Astrology Paradigm, this is a vital part of the journey towards wholeness, and the counterpart to Jung's individuation process.

Important note: the OGP is not necessarily who is best for you in a relationship. Rather, it's who you work out your relationship issues and lessons with. For some, it's clearly not who would be the best type to be with. But in all cases, the qualities and capacities of the OGP will always be what is good for you to develop within yourself and make fully conscious, and take ownership of.

A more expanded view of how to use this material and the cards for manifesting the best possible long-lasting relationship includes the use of the ASC/DSC (Ascendant/Descendant) axis, with particular emphasis on the imagery of the Descendant. More information about the ASC/DSC axis is found in Appendix I.

PROGRESSIVE PROJECTION

There is no intimation here as to whether the projection of the OGP is either good or bad. It's actually entirely natural and appears to be how the psyche is currently operating. Clearly, if we project this image onto someone who is not that way, it will not at all be helpful. This is where full consciousness of the projected archetype can be so empowering. Then we can talk of releasing the projection.

But there is also a type of projection called "progressive" projection. In this case, what a man or woman projects with the imagery of the OGP is actually what the other person actually is, or is attempting to develop confidence in. In this case, the projection is really helpful to the other person, and like attracts like.

And now, it's time to go directly to the 24 cards representing the essence and characteristics of the 12 archetypes of the Masculine and the 12 archetypes of the Feminine, for both men and women, as revealed by the synthesis of the artistic vision of Roy Purcell and the Shamanic Astrology Paradigm.

CHAPTER TEN

The Cards: The Gods and Goddesses

Roy Purcell writes: "Having made a life long journey into the dark recesses of my personality a self actualizing journey through the tools of art and writing, I was at a peak of preparation for this project. I had recently completed a series of fine art projects (portfolios of ink and watercolor paintings and writing) on feminine, masculine and cultural archetypes, when this challenge and opportunity was dropped onto my creative plate. I saw it immediately as a powerful tool of expression of *the soul's journey through the archetypes* and launched myself into it knowing it to be my next necessary creative project.

I had begun a standard tarot deck years before but found it to be impersonal for my tastes. In this approach to understanding the personality through the archetypes, I found a unique expression of the structure and major motivating factors and influences on the personality. This archetypal approach to astrology was, for me, a very humanistic and personal revelation.

The ideas for the cards came to me as fast as I could execute them using the techniques of ink, watercolor and colored pencil. I was in a powerful inspirational flow from which I gained new insights into myself and a better understanding of human nature.

I hope these images and ideas open new doors to your understanding.

Thanks, Daniel Giamario and dedicated group of Shamanic Astrologers, for your insight and work in bringing forth this enlightening philosophical approach to the understanding of the inner journey."

THE GOD ARIES

Warrior/Protector

The Aries God is a man of action dedicated to a noble cause or purpose with the capacity for total commitment: soldiers, warriors, protectors of the established structures of society including family, community, clan and state.

Valued For: Nobility, commitment, speed, strength.

- Fire
- Solar masculine
- Actional
- Non-relational
- Autonomous

Gods and Stories: Aries (Mars), the Kshatriya cast of warriors in India, the Samurai, football quarterbacks, bouncers, soldiers.

Mars in Aries for a woman: Commit to a noble cause or purpose. Do not be dependent on an external partner for this. Take action on your own and be willing to be 100% all-in with your actional commitments. (Refer to Venus in Aries.)

THE GOD TAURUS

Lover/Epicure

The Taurus God explores beauty and aesthetics, personal intimacy as art, and more than any other God, the capacity to receive. As an epicurean, he maximizes pleasure and minimizes pain via pleasure as long as possible, as deep as possible, and in moderation. He is deeply relational but not a culture bearer or pair bonder. Being an earth god, he has little interest in patriarchal conceptions of masculinity.

Valued For: Aesthetics, personal loyalty, capacity for pleasure.

- Earth
- Lunar masculine
- Receptive and receiving
- Relational-personal
- Autonomous

Gods and Stories: The Dagda-Irish Bull God, male courtesan, metro-sexual, epicures of food and fashion.

Mars in Taurus for a woman: Develop the capacity to receive. Give yourself permission to savor and enjoy being in the body. Enjoy your beauty and aesthetics for their own sake. (Refer to Venus in Taurus.)

THE GOD GEMINI

Eternal Youth/Shape-Shifter

The Gemini God is a *puer aeternus* (eternal youth), like Peter Pan. Like the itinerant troubadour minstrel, he is a bringer of magic to all. He is multifaceted in creativity and is dedicated to his freedom and remaining a free electron. A lover of women, he can easily shapeshift to what a woman desires him to be. Above all, he is committed to being beyond the rules of duality and polarity.

Valued For: Curiosity, humor, adaptability, quick mind.

- Air
- Solar masculine
- Actionable and Free
- Socially Relational
- Personally Non-Relational
- Autonomous

Gods and Stories: Hermes, Thoth, Kokopelli, Don Juan, court jester.

Mars in Gemini for the woman: Get in touch with your magical creativity. Be willing to shape shift and enjoy the freedom of being whatever role in life you want to be. Experience life as a playful dance, taking delight in creative expression. (Refer to Venus in Gemini.)

THE GOD CANCER

Father, Provider of Nourishment

The Cancer God is a provider of nourishment. He is dedicated to providing personal, hierarchical, and responsible nourishment to a seed (child, client, student, house, business) to its maturity. Cancer is exclusively a giver, and knows himself through a specific function. He is motivated through the love and compassion of the feeling function (water). His identity is generally based on his family and community. In patriarchal family structure he is the father/provider.

Valued For: Responsibility, committed and caring nourishment, providing emotional support.

- Water
- Lunar masculine
- Giver
- Socially and personally relational in a hierarchical manner
- Actionally responsive to the needs of others
- Vulnerable
- Not autonomous

Gods and Stories: Nurturing fathers and providers, counselors and helpers.

Mars in Cancer for the woman: Develop the capacity to provide nourishment to yourself. Accept your vulnerability. Be willing to re-parent yourself and not expect others to take care of you. (Refer to Venus in Cancer, but do not become more Cancerian except to yourself.)

THE GOD LEO

King, Leading Man

The Leo God is a man of power and authority whose intuitive connection to divinity allows him to create as an end in itself. That willful confidence opens a space of confidence and trust in others. Often his creatorship is expressed as joyful play through which he demonstrates radiant self-love in action. At his best, he models the most positive qualities of a human being to others and will ultimately serve the people.

Valued For: Courage, inspiration, joy, radiant radical self-love.

- Fire
- Solar masculine
- Actional
- Non-relational
- Autonomous

Gods and Stories: Good kings, the leading man, the star, a healthy two year old.

Mars in Leo for a woman: Choose to be an active and intuitive force in creation and leadership. Don't live in the shade of the "great man." Consider the joy of being creator for its own sake. Create your own reality just because you can! (Refer to Venus in Leo.)

THE GOD VIRGO

Priest

The Virgo God is completely dedicated to a sacred work in service to spirit. Historically a renunciate, his attention is not on worldly, secular, or personal affairs. All he does is in service to the integrity and authenticity of his craft and skill. He is impersonal and primarily a giver, with an abnegation of his own personal needs. At his best, he is ultimately in service to Earth Mother.

Valued For: Sense of the sacred, dedication, discriminating precision.

- Earth
- Lunar masculine
- Rational left brain
- Impersonal
- Giver
- Non-relational
- Autonomous

Gods and Stories: Hephaestus (Vulcan), Priest, Ceremonialist.

Mars in Virgo for a woman: Make your emphasis in finding and developing your sacred work your calling. Honor your need for sacred space and your connection to our earth mother. Do not rely on the work or career of your partner. (Refer to Venus in Virgo.)

THE GOD LIBRA

Partner, Husband

The Libra God desires to know himself through another or others. Along with Taurus, he is the most personal of all gods. Historically, his greatest interest is in sustainable, long-term, agreement-based relationships operating within a cultural framework. His intention is "we" not "I." His greatest strength and commitment as a man is to work on a relationship that can result in a non-hierarchical conscious equal partnership and true collaboration. For Libra, relationship itself is a path to God.

Valued For: Being a good partner and how well he is doing in his relationship.

- Air
- Left brain
- Solar and Lunar masculine
- Evolutionary
- Responsive and vulnerable (not autonomous)
- Socially and personally relational

Gods and Stories: Husband/partner, boyfriend, diplomat.

Mars in Libra for the woman: Choose yourself as your best partner. Develop a love for a deep and complete relationship with yourself, even when with a beloved. Do not define yourself through another. (Refer to Venus in Libra but apply it to you.)

THE GOD SCORPIO

Shaman, Sorcerer

The Scorpio God explores the greatest depth and power of life force and aliveness, and aspires for its mastery. The experience of life force is for its own sake and it's his responsibility to respond to this desire. For him, desire is the engine of creation. His authentic response to where the greatest aliveness is, will always supersede mental constraints or social conventions.

Valued For: Depth, passion, eros, power, intensity.

- Water
- Right Brain
- Lunar masculine
- Actional
- Involutionary
- Personally relational for self-interest
- Autonomous

Gods and Stories: Shiva, wild man in the woods, green man, Pan, shaman, sorcerer, wizard, "the bad boys."

Mars in Scorpio for a woman: Make the development of your own *Shakti* (active life force) your priority. Connect with your organic passion and desire without relying on the outside stimulation of exciting and provocative partners. (Refer to Venus in Scorpio to see what you can become.)

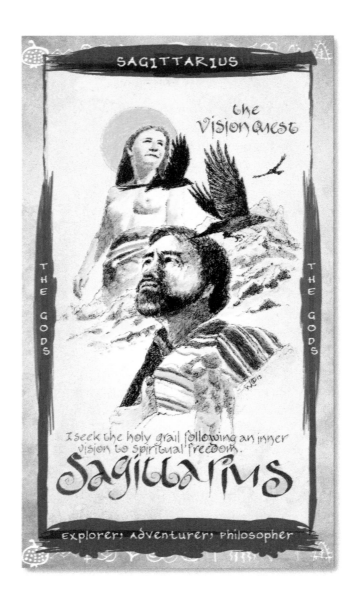

THE GOD SAGITTARIUS

Explorer, Adventurer, Philosopher

The Sagittarius God is dedicated to the quest for meaning and purpose. His greatest joy is the love of truth. His lifestyles are adventure, exploration and philosophy. Traditionally a renunciate, the secular world and personal affairs are a low priority. He loves freedom and has the capacity to change his objectives frequently. The zeal in pursuing this freedom is his way of being in service to spirit.

Valued For: Freedom, adventure, spirituality, truth.

- Fire
- Left brain
- Intuition
- Solar masculine
- Actional
- Evolutionary
- Non-Relational
- Autonomous

Gods and Stories: Labors of Hercules, Jason and the Argonauts, the voyages of Odysseus, "the journey to the East," the Polynesian way finders.

Mars in Sagittarius for a woman: Take on the responsibility of leading your own quest for meaning and purpose. Commit to including freedom and adventure in your life. Do not rely on the visions and inspiration of teachers and partners. (Refer to Venus in Sagittarius as potentially being you.)

CAPRICORN

Capricorn

THE GODS

THE GODS

I am the diplomat, the practical manager
I keep the wheels of society turning

Elder: Responsible Father: Expert

THE GOD CAPRICORN

Elder, Responsible Father, Expert

The Capricorn God is the elder and expert, the responsible one who can hold it together for everyone else. He functions from a hierarchical position and makes the practical decisions for the benefit for the generations to follow, whilst honoring the previous traditions. As a culture bearer he has both the power and respect to carry out the actions for maintaining and then building a new world. Capricorn is primarily a giver with little regard for his own needs as long as he is respected and has a necessary function. He is the least personal of all the gods.

Valued For: His capacities, being responsible, elder knowledge, authority.

- Earth
- Left brain involutionary
- Socially and personally relational from a place of hierarchy
- Lunar masculine
- Actively responsive to the needs of others
- Vulnerable
- Not autonomous

Gods and Stories: Father, Prime Minister, Captain of the ship, Jean Luc Picard ("Star Trek").

Mars in Capricorn for a woman: Take on a practical and responsible activity or project that contributes to the sustainability of the community and society, with a concern for the well-being of future generations. Be willing to take this on with or without being with a partner with these qualities. (See Venus in Capricorn for clues.)

THE GOD AQUARIUS

Innovator, Visionary, Scientist

The Aquarius God is a revolutionary of consciousness. He is committed to universal ideals including egalitarianism, liberty, higher love and progressive idealism. He is a free electron, valuing his radical freedom and personal uniqueness. He stands aloof from mainstream conventions and is committed to his own uniqueness whilst being a champion for everyone else. He is suspicious of superstition, as well as any behaviors or beliefs that are too emotional or riddled with subjectivity.

Valued For: Brilliance, freedom, uniqueness, objectivity, being avant-garde.

- Air
- Solar masculine
- Left brain
- Evolutionary
- Socially and personally transpersonal
- Non-relational
- Autonomous

God and Stories: Avant-garde thinkers, scientist, explorer of consciousness.

Mars in Aquarius for a woman: Be willing to be completely unique, even eccentric. Allow yourself to experience the leading edge and the revolutionary spaces beyond what is considered normal. Develop radical "free electron" spaciousness. (Refer to Venus in Aquarius.)

THE GOD PISCES

Bringer of Ecstasy, Dionysus

The Pisces God is a bringer of ecstatic experience leading to mystical rapture and union. This is the god closest to the archetypal feminine. As a transpersonal giver he loves assisting women (and the feminine in men) in having their wildest, most expansive, most uninhibited experience. Generally a renunciate, he is little interested in worldly or personal life. Mostly committed to the mystical and celestial realities, he emphasizes the experiences that lead to ecstatic experiences for himself as well as being a healer to others.

Valued For: Deep feeling, empathy, compassion, surrender.

- Water
- Lunar masculine
- Right brain
- Involutionary
- Socially and personally transpersonal
- Giver
- Autonomous in service to spirit
- Actively responsive to needs

Gods and Stories: Dionysus and the Maenads, servant of the goddess, the "Year King," the Ayahuasquero, Jesus (early version).

Mars in Pisces for a woman: Open to the transpersonal embrace of the infinite love and nourishment of the masculine aspect of the One Reality and Great Mystery. Be open to receiving a celestial and ecstatic source of nourishment. You are worthy of this healing. (Refer to Venus in Pisces but only in application to yourself.)

ARIES

ARIES

THE GODDESSES

THE GODDESSES

I am the warrior at the base of your psyche

Warrior Amazon

THE GODDESS ARIES

Warrior Amazon

The Aries Goddess is a woman whose identity is based on accomplishment, achievement, and freedom. The Warrior Amazon is a protector and defender totally dedicated to a noble cause or purpose with complete commitment.

Valued For: Nobility, commitment, speed, strength.

- Fire
- Solar Feminine
- Actional
- Non-relational
- Autonomous

Goddesses and Stories: Queen Boudicca, mother bear protecting cubs, Joan of Arc.

Venus in Aries for a man: Make a commitment to a noble cause or purpose not dependent on the inspiration or dictates of a partner. Do not project power and strength onto the feminine. Own your own will. (See Mars in Aries for clues.)

THE GODDESS TAURUS

Venus-Aphrodite Courtesan

The Taurean Goddess explores beauty and aesthetics, personal intimacy as art, and a capacity to receive. As the epicurean goddess, she maximizes pleasure and minimizes pain by ways of pleasure as long as possible, as deep as possible, and with sufficient moderation to not create any pain. She's deeply relational, but not a family oriented culture-bearer or pair-bonder.

Valued For: Beauty and aesthetics, personal loyalty, capacity to receive

- Earth
- Lunar Feminine
- Receptive and receiving
- Relational-personal
- Autonomous

Goddesses and Stories: Venus-Aphrodite, Persephone (before her abduction), Courtesans and Hetaeras

---

Venus in Taurus for a man: Place greater attention on your physical embodiment, allowing yourself to emphasize your own capacity to enjoy *intimacy as art*. Do not be overly seduced or distracted or give your power away to the beauty of women. (See Mars in Taurus for clues.)

THE GODDESS GEMINI

Eternal Youth

The Gemini Goddess is a *puella aeterna* (eternal youth), spirit girl and female Peter Pan. Like the itinerant circus/carnival performer, she is multifaceted in creativity and dedicated to freedom and remaining a free electron. Her mission, through creative freedom, is to bring magic to the world.

Valued For: Curiosity, humor, adaptability, quick mind.

- Air
- Solar and Lunar Feminine
- Actional and free
- Socially relational, personally non-relational
- Autonomous

Goddesses and Stories: The Puella Aeterna, Iris (the Rainbow Goddess), female Heyokah, female Don Juan (Doña Juanita?)

Venus in Gemini for a man: Get in touch with your creative, magical, and playful side. Allow yourself to be an eternal youth (*puer aeternus)*. Do not rely on your partner or women as necessary for your inspiration. (See Mars in Gemini for clues.)

THE GODDESS CANCER

Great Mother

The Cancer Goddess is a mother-nurturer. She is dedicated to providing personal, hierarchical, and responsible nourishment to a seed (child, client, student, etc.) to its maturity. She is exclusively a giver, and knows herself through a specific function of some kind. She is motivated by the love and compassion gained through the feeling function (water). Her identity is generally based on her family and community.

Valued For: Responsibility, caring nourishment, providing emotional support.

- Water
- Lunar Feminine
- Socially and personally relational in a hierarchical way
- Actively responsive to needs of others
- Vulnerable, not autonomous

Goddesses and Stories: Mother goddesses, Mother Mary, Great Mother/ Great Mystery.

Venus in Cancer for a man: Develop the capacity to provide nourishment to yourself. See your vulnerability and longing for nurturing as a strength. Be willing to take responsibility for re-parenting yourself. Above all, do not project the need for this nourishment onto a partner. (See Mars in Cancer for clues, but apply it to yourself, not others.)

THE GODDESS LEO

Amazon Queen

The Leo Goddess is a woman whose identity is based on accomplishment, achievement, and freedom. The Leo Amazon queen is a leader and vision carrier. Her capacity to create with confidence opens the space for confidence and freedom in others. She is guided by an intuitive connection to the universal will coming directly from divinity. Often this creatorship is expressed as joyful play.

Valued For: Radiant radical self-love, courage, inspiration, joy.

- Fire
- Right Brain
- Solar Feminine
- Actional
- Non relational
- Autonomous

Goddesses and Stories: The Queen, the leading woman, the star, the healthy two year old.

Venus in Leo for a man: Be the creator of your own reality and the vision carrier of your own life. Be willing to actively create for its own sake, for the joy of it. Do not project these qualities onto a solar feminine in order to be inspired. (See Mars in Leo for clues.)

THE GODDESS VIRGO

Priestess

The Virgo Goddess is a priestess, a woman whose highest priority is commitment to a Sacred Work in service to spirit. Historically a renunciate, her attention is not on worldly, secular, or personal affairs. She is "virgin," meaning, one unto herself and not defined through a husband or secular family. Her domain is that of Earth Mother and the rhythm and cycles of women's sacred mysteries. Primarily a giver and impersonal, her inviolate commitment is in maintaining the integrity of the patterning of the web of life.

Valued For: Honoring of sacred space, dedication, a sense of the sacred and discriminating precision.

- Earth
- Left Brain
- Lunar feminine
- Rational
- Impersonal
- Giver
- Non-relational
- Autonomous

Goddesses and Stories: High priestesses, Hestia/Vesta, Demeter, Gaia, Spider Woman, sisters of Wyrdd.

Venus in Virgo for a man: Make your calling or your *sacred work* your priority. Develop a relationship with the natural world, the earth, the stones, the landscape, the sky, etc. Find your own sacred space. Do not expect any woman to totally "get" what you are doing. (See Mars in Virgo for clues.)

THE GODDESS LIBRA

Partner, Wife

The Libra Goddess desires to know herself through another or others. Along with Taurus, she is the most personal of all goddesses. Historically, her greatest interest is in sustainable, long term, agreement based relationships, operating within a cultural framework. Her intention is "we" not "I." At this time in history she aspires for non-hierarchical conscious equal partnership and true collaboration. For her, relationship itself is a path to God.

Valued For: Her relational skills and how well she is doing in a relationship.

- Air
- Solar and Lunar Feminine
- Left brain
- Evolutionary
- Responsive and vulnerable
- Not autonomous
- Socially and personally relational

Goddesses and Stories: Hera/Juno, the wife, the girlfriend, the diplomat.

Venus in Libra for a man: Become your own best partner. Love being in relationship with yourself as even better than any possible external partner. Never define who you are by who you are with. (See Mars in Libra but apply it to yourself, not others.)

THE GODDESS SCORPIO

Sorceress, Medicine Woman

The Scorpio Goddess is the sorceress/witch, meaning the goddess closest to the great depth and power of the feminine. Sorceress means her connection to and mastery of life force. She explores life force and maximum aliveness for its own sake. She has the capacity and the responsibility to explore and master the farthest extremes of aliveness and passion. She is deeply embodied in earth and water. For her, desire is the engine of creation.

Valued For: Depth, passion, eros, power, intensity.

- Water
- Lunar Feminine
- Right brain
- Actional
- Involutionary
- Personally relational for self-interest
- Autonomous

Goddesses and Stories: Shakti, Kali, Hecate, Cretan Snake Goddess, Tantrika, Ereshkigal.

Venus in Scorpio for a man: Make the development of your own physical and emotional passion and power your priority. Find an expression in your life for that passion. Be willing to feel deeply everything that you feel. Do not be distracted or addicted to external sources of stimulation, particularly *shakti dominant* women. (See Mars in Scorpio for clues.)

THE GODDESS SAGITTARIUS

Vision Quest Amazon

The Sagittarius Goddess is a woman whose identity is based upon her achievements, accomplishments and freedom. The motive of the Sagittarian Vision Quest Amazon is to seek the truth, the quest for the meaning and purpose of life, with the ultimate goal of enlightenment and self-realization. Her lifestyles are adventure, exploration and philosophy. She knows that this is the best way to be in service to spirit.

Valued For: Freedom, adventurousness, spirituality, truthfulness.

- Fire
- Solar Feminine
- Right brain
- Intuition
- Evolutionary
- Actional
- Non-relational
- Autonomous

Goddesses and Stories: Tara, Sophia, Sacajawea.

Venus in Sagittarius for a man: Take responsibility for leading your own vision quest for meaning and purpose. Develop your capacity for exploration and adventure on your own. Don't rely on the direction and guidance of your partner or adventurous and inspiring women. (See Mars in Sagittarius for clues.)

THE GODDESS CAPRICORN

Elder, Grandmother, Empress

The Capricorn Goddess is the elder and expert, the responsible one who can hold it together for everyone else. She sits in the circle of grandmothers and makes the practical decisions for the benefit of the seven generations to follow. As a culture bearer, she has both the power and respect to carry out the practical decisions for maintaining and then building a new world. She is primarily a giver with little regard for her own needs as long as she is respected and has a necessary function. She is the least personal of all the goddesses.

Valued For: Her capacities, responsibilities, elder knowledge, authority.

- Earth
- Lunar Feminine
- Left brain
- Involutionary
- Socially and personally relational from a place of hierarchy
- Actively responsive to the needs of others
- Vulnerable
- Not autonomous

Goddesses and Stories: Council of Elders, Circle of Grandmothers, responsible mother, manager, businesswoman, supermom.

Venus in Capricorn for a man: Take responsibility for developing a practical project or contribution that benefits the community and society with future generations in mind. Honor your own wisdom and don't rely on partners that are there to teach you, parent you, or support you. (See Mars in Capricorn for clues.)

T H E GODDESS AQUARIUS

Egalitarian, Visionary, Innovator

The Aquarius Goddess is the Goddess of democracy. Being an innovator and visionary, she is committed to universal ideals including egalitarianism, liberty, higher love and progressive idealism. She is a free electron, valuing her radical freedom and personal uniqueness. She is a revolutionary in thought and is aloof from mainstream conventions. Not only is she fiercely committed to her own uniqueness but is also a champion for everyone else's.

Valued For: Brilliance, freedom, uniqueness, avant-garde personality, objectivity.

- Air
- Solar Feminine
- Left brain
- Evolutionary
- Socially and personally transpersonal
- Non-relational
- Autonomous

Goddesses and Stories: The Goddess of Reason, Goddess of Democracy, Statue of Liberty, scientist, explorer of consciousness, Kuan Yin (along with Pisces).

Venus in Aquarius for a man: Be willing to explore your own uniqueness and even eccentricity. Explore the leading edges of your possibilities. Be open to something other than normal. Develop ease and comfort in your freedom and spaciousness. Don't rely on living your life through unusual, eccentric and free spirited women. (See Mars in Aquarius for clues.)

THE GODDESS PISCES

Transcendent Love, Great Mother/Great Mystery

The Pisces Goddess is committed to helping and healing everyone. Because of her deep connection to the feeling function and being a giver she has the greatest capacity to feel into the grief, sorrow and suffering of humanity. Being self-abnegated and transpersonal, without her own boundaries or personal needs (other than being of help to others), she is indiscriminate in her desire and capacity to help. Throughout history she is the compassionate and nonjudgmental healing energy of the sacred feminine.

Valued For: Compassion, empathy, healing, selfless love.

- Water
- Lunar Feminine
- Right brain
- Involutionary
- Socially and personally transpersonal
- Giver
- Autonomous in service to spirit
- Actively responsive to needs

Goddesses and Stories: Our Lady of Guadalupe, Mother Mary, Great Mother/Great Mystery, Diksha, Kuan Yin (along with Aquarius).

Venus in Pisces for a man: Open yourself to the transpersonal and universal embrace of the loving essence of Great Mystery in her female expression, receiving unconditional nourishment from that "one woman." Do not project this longing onto any individual. (See Mars in Pisces for clues, but for yourself, not others.)

CHAPTER ELEVEN

The Twelve Mystery Schools

In the use of the divination card deck, often people will ask: "Where is the card for the Sun?" As explained throughout this book, the Shamanic Astrology Paradigm has de-emphasized Sun signs.

Instead, Shamanic Astrology emphasizes what are called the Twelve Mystery Schools. There is a card for each one of them. The meaning and intent of each mystery school is further elaborated in this chapter. These meanings and intentions can be applied to any part of the chart. There is, of course, no good or bad, right or wrong, higher or lower, or more evolved or less evolved.

However, if applied to the Moon, then it's potentially regressive, symbolizing skills and experiences that have already been your core identity, and which you are moving away from. Applied to other parts of the chart, the meanings and intentions are progressive, likened to the set of instructions for current life intent.

Because of the significant emphasis on the importance of the Venus and Mars placements, 24 cards for Mars and Venus have been provided with much of the mystery school teachings built in. Should you draw both at the same time, for example: Taurus Mystery School and Mars or Venus in Taurus, there would certainly be no ambiguity about what needs to be worked on now. However, if your natal Moon is in Taurus, the same cards could suggest looking at where you are regressively identified.

WHAT IS A MYSTERY SCHOOL?

The *mystery* in the expression *mystery school* originally and traditionally refers to a special gnosis or a secret wisdom. Such schools have been dedicated to explore the secrets of Life and to learn the secrets of this hidden knowledge. Only sincere students displaying a desire for this knowledge and then meeting certain tests were considered worthy of being introduced to these mysteries. Historically there has always been an initiatory dimension to a mystery school. Clearly a mystery school is NOT a secular or mainstream form of education.

The Shamanic Astrology Mystery School (SAMS) has included this perennial understanding of a mystery school with the concept of "Great Mystery," as the suggested and preferred way of designating the Ultimate Reality of Existence. Hermeticists often use the terms "the One Reality" or sometimes "The Pattern" to refer to this same "Great Mystery." In India, the well-known mantra: "I Am THAT, Thou art THAT, all THIS is THAT" also refers to this same "Great Mystery."

In these times, at the *Turning Of The Ages*, a considerably larger percentage of people can gain access to the knowledge and experience of "Great Mystery," as global humanity is moving beyond class and hierarchy. The requirement to have special priest/priestess elites high above everyone else and keeping secrets for no other reason than dominance and control is being rightfully exposed. Nevertheless, sincerity, intelligence, a willingness to study, and the courage to undergo an initiatory process remain integral parts of the Shamanic Astrology Mystery School.

The use of "mystery school" as a designation for the twelve signs refers to the fact that throughout history, the twelve signs can be thought of as schools of life, each with a unique and specific function and purpose. Often, in the past, only elites, priests, and rulers were involved in the development of these schools and the determination as to which ones were important. Often, they only revealed the outer teachings and particularly the parts that served them best.

The Twelve Mystery School cards in the Divination Deck revealed in the next chapter includes many of the historical, and in some ways, eternal teachings contained in these schools of life, as well as clues suggesting how they have evolved and are ever-changing in their content. The intent here is to show how they can serve the needs of global humanity at this time in history: the *Turning Of The Ages*. The hope is that these teachings become more generally known and increasingly accessible to anyone who is genuinely open and interested, without judgments, to explore and investigate these mysteries. And then, to demonstrate a willingness to inquire into these matters without the overlays of consensus reality and cultural relativity.

Neptune

Possibilities

empbiness is the receptacle who's
of all wisdom
dreamtime - the mystical realms

INITIATIONS

INITIATIONS

CHAPTER TWELVE

The Cards: The Twelve Mystery Schools

Additional information about the Twelve Mystery Schools follows alongside the beautiful illustrations by Roy Purcell who has artfully tapped into their essence.

Each mystery school has its own way and approach to a fully realized life, its own view and definiton of so-called "enlightenment." Often self realization and enlightenment are used interchangeably.

The assumption is that each mystery school has its own unique way of fulfilling its intention to achieve a fully realized life. The following descriptions of each school cover the twelve ways of fulfilling this intention by looking at the valuable categories of dharma and yoga.

Dharma can be understood within the context of the Shamanic Astrology Paradigm as referring to the "intent" for current life purpose as symbolized by the Ascendant in combination with the house position of the North Node, and then executed by the Goddess or God symbolized by a man's Mars or a woman's Venus. This is augmented by the archetypal mysteries seen through the symbol of Jupiter by sign. Dharma is the "intended" way of life that is our duty to perform sooner or later. This is often not the path of least resistance.

Yoga references techniques or practices that best complement and assist the accomplishment of one of the twelve dharmas. Though often defined as a practice to attain union, here it is seen as a specific yoga or practice designed to fulfill the intentions toward a fully realized life. A great number of practices can thus assist one in accomplishing a specific dharma including marriage or martial arts.

ARIES

Culture Bearer

The Aries Mystery School is the defender and protector of the ways of life that contribute to the sustainability of culture from one generation to the next. Aries is characterized by a total, black and white commitment to a noble cause or purpose. They protect the established order, be it family, team, clan, state, or country.

- Fire
- Masculine
- Evolutionary
- Actional
- Non relational

Characterized by: Action, competition, doing (not being), nobility of purpose, honor, righteousness, valour.

Historical Themes and Stories: Kshatriya protecting the priesthood (Brahmans), the Samurai in service to a Lord, soldiers and warriors, generals and quarterbacks.

Spiritual Path (Dharma): Householder, warrior-protector, commitment as the foundation for true freedom.

Yogas: Martial arts, physical fitness, pursuit of excellence, nobility of character, codes of conduct with commitment to moral and social codes, dedicated service to the noble cause.

TAURUS

Self-Interest

The Taurus Mystery School explores the widest possibilities of pleasure and sensation in the body, for its own sake. Related to epicureanism, it seeks to maximize pleasure and minimize pain through: endurance—pleasure as long as possible, intensity—pleasure as deep as possible, moderation—never going to the point resulting in pain. Taurus also explores authentic receivership, by knowing what is good and gifting a giver with the gift of receiving. This Mystery School explores deep personal intimacy as art, not as a means of reproduction, or the maintaining of a marriage, as with culture bearers. Taurus brings spirit into matter in order to enjoy it.

- Earth
- Feminine
- Involutionary
- Personal
- Relational

Characterized by: Receptive receiving, being (not doing), pleasure for its own sake.

Historical Themes and Stories: Courtesans and Hetaeras, artists, models, cooks, epicures, artists.

Spiritual Path (Dharma): Epicureanism, the aim of which is to maximize pleasure and minimize pain. To celebrate the fullness and the pleasure of spirit in the senses, with the capacity to fully and completely savor the present moment.

Yogas: Hatha Yoga, Partner Yoga, Red Tantra Yoga, intimacy as art, the pleasure of creating art.

GEMINI

In Service to Spirit

The Gemini Mystery School is dedicated to exploring the infinite highways and byways of the dance of duality and polarity that characterize the human experience. By employing all available circuits of the mind, Gemini loves all forms of networking and communication that creates space for even more connections. Gemini ultimately uses the mind to go beyond the apparent confines of duality and polarity. With this, Gemini's service to spirit is that the mind is free to serve spirit by knowing that the mind cannot know it all, and can thus see the humor in the dance of life.

- Air
- Masculine
- Evolutionary
- Actionable and free
- Socially relational, personally non-relational

Characterized by: Versatility, curiosity, changeability, irreverence, humor, networking within and beyond duality and polarity.

Historical Themes and Stories: Tricksters, court jesters, story tellers, shape-shifters, troubadour minstrels, "the Fool" from the Tarot.

Spiritual Path (Dharma): To use the mind to go beyond the limits of the mind. This is a pathway beyond duality and polarity.

Yogas: Zen, Aikido, satire, gymnastics and acrobatics, alchemy, song, dance, story-telling, magic, "Crazy Wisdom."

CANCER

Culture Bearer

The Cancer Mystery School develops the forms and structures that sustain home, family, clan, community, and country over time, honoring the ancestors and nourishing the generations to come. Its actions are hierarchical, such as parent to child and teacher to student. Whether patriarchal or matriarchal, Cancer is motivated by the feeling function, personal love, and a response to wherever the need for nourishment is found. At its best, Cancer can see all of humanity as one family.

- Water
- Feminine
- Involutionary
- Hierarchically Relational
- Actively Responsive

Characterized by: Taking care of others, responsibility, providing nourishment in home and community, empathy.

Historical Themes and Stories: The personal and human aspects of "mothering" in both women and men.

Spiritual Path (Dharma): To investigate and then uphold the traditions and institutions that provide security and long-lasting stability and nourishment to the children, family and community.

Yogas: Karma Yoga, householder, successfully raising a family, the nurturing and helping of others.

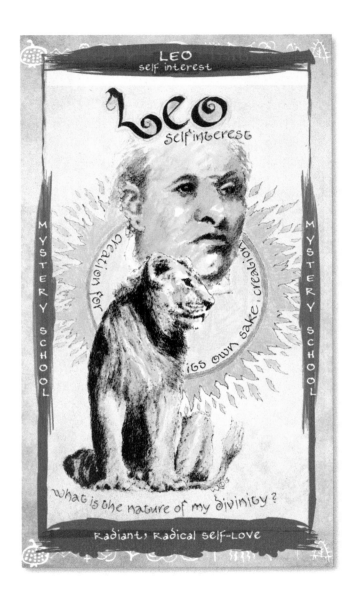

LEO

Self-Interest

The Leo Mystery School explores the activities and willful actions of pure creation, for its own sake, as an end in itself. These expressions of creation are exemplified by courage, and a childlike joyfulness and innocence, as if one is directly connected with divinity. At best, Leo generously inspires others to be everything they can be.

- Fire
- Masculine
- Evolutionary
- Actional
- Non-relational

Characterized by: Joy, confidence, audacity, centered-on-self generosity, creation for its own sake.

Historical Themes and Stories: Kings, Queens, vision carriers, creators, stars.

Spiritual Path (Dharma): The realization of sovereignty and autonomy and thereby the identity with divinity, development of radiant and radical self-love, the demonstration of one's creatorship.

Yogas: Inspired leadership, Raja Yoga, Vision carrier.

VIRGO

In Service to Spirit

The Virgo Mystery School is dedicated to exploring the sacredness of the manifest creation. It perceives and then works with the pattern of all life, the universe of Gaia or Earth Mother, including all the connections that exist between "As Above, So Below." Virgo's dedication is to uphold the sacredness of this pattern, and then to create sacred space in all possible ways. Generally a renunciate path, essentially impersonal and self-abnegated, its connection is with and in service to spirit and the web of life. Virgo brings spirit into matter in order to worship it and honor its sacredness.

- Earth
- Feminine
- Involutionary
- Impersonal
- Non-relational

Characterized by: Discrimination, precision, pattern recognition, autonomy, sacred service aligned with Earth Mother.

Historical Themes and Stories: Priest and Priestesses, sacred work, themes of renunciation, "women's mysteries."

Spiritual Path (Dharma): Directly cognizing and comprehending the sacred pattern or web of life, and then being in alignment with it.

Yogas: Renunciate, stoicism, hygiene. right diet, inquiry, adherence to pattern, creation of ceremony and ritual, Bhakti yoga.

LIBRA

Culture Bearer

The Libra Mystery School develops the forms and structures that create sustainable personal partnerships and relationships over time. In the history of humanity, it's Libra that has created the varieties of pair-bonding and marriage formats, as well as other collaborative relationships. Its intent is to know oneself through the other or others. At its best, Libra aspires for non-hierarchical conscious equal partnerships, not the hierarchical roles found in patriarchy.

- Air
- Masculine
- Evolutionary
- Personal
- Relational

Characterized by: Personalness, social awareness, relational ideals, sustainable non-hierarchical conscious equal partnerships.

Historical Themes and Stories: Husbands and wives, Rama and Sita, consensus decision making, diplomacy.

Spiritual Path (Dharma): The focus on personal relationships with other human beings and to have the experience of being loved just for "you."

Yogas: Marriage, mediation, relationship as a path to God, mirroring, collaboration.

SCORPIO

Self-Interest

The Scorpio Mystery School explores the many ways of experiencing the greatest possibilities of aliveness, passion, and life force. It has the courage to go beyond any perceived edge that constrains even greater aliveness. This exploration uses the physical and emotional component of the human experience for its own sake, and as an end in itself. For Scorpio, this desire is the engine of creation. At its best, Scorpio can experience the maximum capacities of a human being to plug in to Ananda, or the greatest bliss that is possible in the body and soul.

- Water
- Feminine
- Involutionary
- Personally relational
- Actional

Characterized by: Intensity, depth, passion, eros, maximum aliveness for its own sake.

Historical Themes and Stories: Shakti and Shiva, sorceress witch, shamans and wizards, alchemy, nuclear power.

Spiritual Path (Dharma): To explore the right use of will and engagement with power, to plug directly into the infinite energy of Great Mystery.

Yogas: Tantra yoga, Kundalini Yoga, many earth based Shamanic practices, breathwork.

SAGITTARIUS
service to spirit

service to spirit

Sagittarius

what is the nature of truth?
the holy grail of life? that is my
quest!

quest for meaning,
purpose and truth

MYSTERY SCHOOL

MYSTERY SCHOOL

SAGITTARIUS

In Service to Spirit

The Sagittarius Mystery School is dedicated to the exploration of meaning and purpose. Its themes are generally adventure, exploration and philosophy. "To boldly go where no one has gone before." Sagittarius believes that the greatest way to be in service to spirit is to attend to one's own freedom and liberation first. Generally a renunciate and non-secular, Sagittarius values freedom with perpetual change and growth. At its best, Sagittarius ultimately is a lover of Truth, not ideals of Truth.

- Fire
- Masculine
- Evolutionary
- Actional
- Non-relational

Characterized by: Enthusiasm, adventure, freedom, expansion; quest for meaning, purpose and truth.

Historical Themes and Stories: The labors of Hercules, Jason and the Argonauts, the Lewis and Clark expeditions, "Journey to the East," the original story of Tara.

Spiritual Path (Dharma): To go boldly into new territory, to question all dogma and crystallizations of truth.

Yogas: Vision quests, wayfaring, the rite of "initiation" itself, philosophy, inquiry.

CAPRICORN

Culture Bearer

The Capricorn Mystery School develops the forms and structures that sustain home, family, clan, community, and country over time, honoring the ancestors and creating the practical traditions and institutions for the generations to come. Its actions are hierarchical, such as parent to child and teacher to student. Capricorn is motivated by practical and responsible outcomes. As an Earth (Sensation Function) Mystery School, its concern is for what works. Capricorn brings spirit into matter in order to manage it. At its best, it's concerned for the future benefit of the earth itself and of all humanity. This is not to be confused with patriarchal ideas about Capricorn.

- Earth
- Feminine
- Involutionary
- Hierarchically Relational
- Actional

Characterized by: Responsibility, holding it together for others, the least personal of all Mystery Schools.

Historical Themes and Stories: Council of elders, Circle of Grandmothers, prime ministers, "fathering" in both men and women.

Spiritual Path (Dharma): To discover, understand and manage the material plane; mastering the operating manual of objective reality for the benefit and sustainability of the world.

Yogas: Sacred geometry, architecture, Ashtanga yoga, Karma yoga, householder, director.

AQUARIUS
self interest

cosmic visionary ~universal free spirit

MYSTERY SCHOOL

MYSTERY SCHOOL

Aquarius

exploration of consciousness
for its ownsake

AQUARIUS

Self-Interest

The Aquarius Mystery School explores the widest possibilities of the expansion of consciousness for its own sake, and as an end in itself. Aquarius is dedicated to unlimited freedom and unbounded spaciousness. In the human realm, it's always resonant with innovation, uniqueness, eccentricity, and the avant-garde. Aquarius has little interest in consensus realities or ordinary conventions. At its best, it aspires to see what others can't see, and then to be established in the place of the ultimate witness, the "I behind the I." This is ultimate objectivity.

- Air
- Masculine
- Evolutionary
- Non-relational
- Impersonal

Characterized by: Spaciousness, uniqueness, freedom, brilliance, objectivity; exploration of consciousness for its own sake.

Historical Themes and Stories: Devic kingdom and the realm of faerie, the "prime directive" (science fiction theme), mad scientist.

Spiritual Path (Dharma): To courageously keep expanding the vision of possibilities, to come up with innovations and to see the ways that others do not see, to always question conformity to the herd and the tyranny of consensus reality.

Yogas: Vipassana, Gyana Yoga, the scientific method, willingness to be yourself.

PISCES

In Service to Spirit

The Pisces Mystery School is dedicated to exploring the heart and poignancy of the human experience. From a transpersonal perspective, Pisces has the capacity to feel and sense into where grief, sorrow, and suffering resides, and then to develop effective ways to help and heal everyone. Generally a renunciate path, Pisces can operate from a self-abnegated and indiscriminate empathy for all. At its best, Pisces can genuinely feel the suffering and unfulfillment of others, but simultaneously can give to whomever is suffering permission to have their own predicament.

- Water
- Feminine
- Involutionary
- Transpersonal
- Actively responsive

Characterized by: Compassion, empathy, desire to help, mystical quality.

Historical Themes and Stories: Healers, world servers, mystics, savior.

Spiritual Path (Dharma): Mystical union with the heart of the universe, unconditional love of great mystery, abnegation of the self; to develop ways of experiencing ecstatic states without surrendering to addiction and the loss of capacity to function in the world with a healthy egoic structure.

Yogas: Bhakti Yoga, Seva, Deeksha, the path of the Bodhisattva, volunteerism, selfless service, devotion, renunciate, ecstatic ceremony.

Daniel Giamario and Jack Roberts with Irish dolmen
Photo by Cristina Moreira

End Notes

1 *The Bhagavad Gita,* "The Song of the Bhagavan," often referred to as simply the Gita, is a 700-verse scripture that is part of the Hindu epic Mahabharata.

2 Dharma is the *intended* way of life that is our duty to perform, sooner or later. This is often not the path of least resistance. For more, go to **http://shamanicastrology.com/twelve-paths-of-spirituality.**

3 "Wild Thyme," written by Paul Kantner, Jefferson Airplane, 1967 album *After Bathing at Baxter's.*

4 Cultural creative has the meaning of better health, lower consumption, more spirituality as opposed to religiosity, more respect for the earth and the diversity within it. Sherry Ruth Anderson and Paul Ray in their book, *The Cultural Creatives: How 50 Million People Are Changing the World*, discuss how the older, more traditional roles for men and women not only don't work, but are nowhere close to the whole story.

5 The Sacred Marriage is elaborated upon in Chapter Nine as well as in subsequent writings that can be found at **http://shamanicastrology.com**.

6 On the meaning of mandala – the way I'm using mandala is as a circular representation of all possibilities; a useful, holistic description of all the possibilities inherent in anything which is being represented.

7 The word "soul" is used here to denote the more common use of the word as a person or individual, not the more technical use of the word soul (along with spirit) as differentiated in archetypal psychology – soul being feminine and spirit being masculine, much like anima and animus.

8 "Essence," written by Steve Kilbey, The Church, 1990 album *Gold Afternoon Fix.*

9 "The Amazon Problem," p 62, by Rene Malamud, in the book, *Facing the Gods*, edited by James Hillman.

Callanish
Photo by Gavin Drummond

Appendix I

The following is taken from *The Shamanic Astrology Handbook* by Daniel Giamario with Cayelin K Castell, pages 116-121.

The Relationship Axis
(The First and Seventh House Axis)

The relationship axis answers the questions: Why in the world would you even want to be in a relationship? What is the current life relationship intent? What is a person's bottom line for the type of experience they desire in a relationship?

The culture we were born into has only two recognized relationship models. One is the family model, where the reason people get married is to bring a family in for the continuity of the generations to follow, and until death do us part. The other model is based on romantic imagery, the quest for the soul mate, couple consciousness, finding "the one." We tend to believe if we could find the right partner, everything would be magical and great. There are, as I will show, other valid options besides these two.

The relationship axis is determined by what Rising Sign a person has. For example, if a person has Leo Rising, they are on the Leo/ Aquarius axis. If a person has Aries Rising, they are on the Aries/Libra axis and so on. The relationship axis is one of the most important parts of the chart. The Rising Sign represents the Personal Identity Project.

The Seventh House Descendant represents the Partnership Project, or what doorway a person goes through to experience partnership. Hence, the relationship between the first and seventh house, the Ascendant and Descendant is what is called the relationship axis. Remember, we are using the Whole Sign House System, so the Ascendant and Descendant are located in the First House and the Seventh House and do not define the cusps of those houses.

TAURUS/SCORPIO AXIS

This is the path of the "Sacred Consort," or tantra. The bottom line is, life force energy itself. This path has to do with sexuality and life force energy. Those on the Taurus/Scorpio axis know they are in the right relationship, if their batteries are getting charged or if there is an increase in life force energy. If they are not having this experience in connection with their relationship they are probably in the wrong one. Taurus/Scorpio is not a giver place. It is not a place where one is drained at the end. The relationship intent is to fully experience the current of life with the partner, to be fully into the current of life, or on the tantric path. If a person has Taurus or Scorpio Moon, it represents the relationship intent in the past, and is not necessarily the relationship intent for the current life, unless they have Taurus or Scorpio Rising.

If one or both partners in a marriage are on the Taurus/Scorpio axis it is essential to the health of the marriage that they have an energizing sex life, and are experiencing an increase in life force energy in connection with each other. Even if the marriage is working nicely on many other levels, such as a strong commitment to each other, many of the same intellectual interests, financial security and an ability to get along on day-to-day matters, if the sex isn't good anymore, and they aren't working on it, the commitment to the marriage ultimately has been broken.

Waiting several years to do something about it is far above and beyond the call of duty, because the reason these two people are in a relationship is to profoundly experience life force energy. The purpose of marriage on this axis is to experience the tantric path through the methodology or modality of primary partnership.

When looking at the issue of sexuality, it seems human beings can be divided up into three categories, about one third each. This is not an exact division, nor does it have to do with gender, but this example helps to illustrate how the different paths of relationship can manifest.

One third of human beings are naturally pair bonders for life, or would like to be. Another one third of human beings are into serial monogamy. In this case, serial monogamy describes someone who can only be fully intimate with one person at a time, but they tend to have a series of relationships. In these speeded up times, an intimate relationship may last only two weeks or two years. However, the reality is, the serial monogamist is not comfortable being with more than one person at a time.

Lastly, we have one third of human beings who are fully capable of being intimate with more than one person at a time. In this category a person could be an insensitive, exploitive, promiscuous person, or they could be a person with a great deal of integrity, intending that every connection they have is a healing situation, or they are involved with several other partners, who like themselves, are wanting to experience divinity by sharing their life force energy. It is important to know that all of these categories can be done well, or done poorly.

The Taurus/Scorpio path can express in all three categories, but usually does not show up as a pair bonder primary partnership. However, if someone has a Libra Moon, they have a past life history that was a pair bonder for life. If the Libra Moon now has the Taurus/Scorpio axis they will probably want to explore the tantric realms within the context of a pair bonding situation, and take the life force energy to its highest expression with their partner.

Conversely, if someone has an Aries Moon, Gemini Sun, Scorpio Rising, and Taurus on the seventh, it is extremely unlikely they will choose marriage to one person. The more likely situation, in a positive expression, is for them to become the tantra teacher, or the tantrika, or the person who has lots of connections done well.

The important point here is, understanding how a person chooses to express their relationship axis is largely dependent upon other factors found on the natal chart. This means that it is important to look at other factors, especially the Moon, Venus and Mars placements, to get the full picture of relationship intent.

GEMINI/SAGITTARIUS AXIS

Sagittarius/Gemini as a relationship axis does not look like a tradition-al couple. This relationship path is best described by the quest mate or the trail mate. The main intent here is to be with someone who supports their spiritual quest and an independent search for the truth. It is helpful if the partner is on a similar or the same quest, but it is not absolutely necessary as long as they support their partner's spiritual quest. This is also the type of relationship that might show up as two people with independent careers, living in separate towns, and only getting together on the weekends.

This relationship path is about having a lot of space and freedom. If a person on this relationship path is experiencing a sense of space, a sense of freedom, and as sense of support for their spiritual quest then it is a healthy relationship for the Sagittarius or Gemini Rising. Obviously this is a rela-tionship path not previously recognized or honored by consensus reality.

PISCES/VIRGO AXIS

This is the path of the helpmate. The bottom line for Pisces/Virgo is finding someone who is equally dedicated to a sacred work. If a person is on the Virgo/Pisces axis and they are in a relationship they are obsessed with, to the point that the other person is all they think about, to the detriment of "the work;" it is the wrong relationship. The point of the Pisces/Virgo axis is to have a partner that is equally dedicated to the work. The partner doesn't have to do the same work, but they must have the same attitude about "the work." However, it is ideal if both partners are committed to the same work.

Jung defines the work, as when a person gets up in the morning, and they absolutely know what they are doing is what they were born to do. When a person knows what the work is for them, it is far more important than fame, position, money, security, or any of the rest of it.

People who survive AIDS are the ones who know what the work is for them, because they have a sense of purpose; they know what they are contributing. The work is more important than the relationship itself. Any relationship that distracts Pisces/Virgo from knowledge of the work, or doing the work, is an inappropriate relationship. Ideally, the relationship supports the work, and the work they are doing is something they really love to do.

LIBRA/ARIES AXIS

On the Aries/Libra axis, relationship is the path to God. This has been referred to as the search for the soul mate, or couple consciousness, and was expressed in the idea that if a person could just find the right partner, they would live a happy and fulfilled life. Images such as riding off into the sunset and living happily ever after have fed this concept.

More accurately and realistically Aries/Libra is the creative engagement of partnership. It is through the interaction with the partner that assists Aries/Libra in learning more about who they are. The Aries/ Libra axis is designed to do the most processing with their partner. That means it is just as good to have a huge argument as to have everything in happiness and bliss, because that is part of the learning process.

Libra Rising comes into the life to take the training of partnership and relationship. The joke on Libra Rising is, they present themselves to the world as being really interested in conscious relationship, but they automatically draw Aries on the seventh house. The joke is the type of partner most likely to come in, is the type least likely to be interested in processing the relationship.

The Aries type is the independent free spirit; the man or woman who knows who they are. Then we might logically ask; why would a person ostensibly interested in relationship draw the type that isn't? Ultimately, this is how the Libra Rising person learns. If they drew someone who was already knowledgeable about relationship, there wouldn't be a learning process.

For Libra/Aries the most potent path to learn more about one's self is through conscious equal partnership. It doesn't mean the Libra/ Aries person is home free when they find a partner. What it does mean is, through constant creative interchanges with equals, they learn more about themselves. Another way of saying it is: the partner is the mantra. In meditation, the instruction is, if you are off the mantra, go back to the mantra. For the Libra/Aries path, if you are off the partner, go back to the partner. It is a process of constantly refining the awareness through interaction with a partner.

Even though the relationship intent is the same for Aries Rising and Libra Rising, there is still a slight difference between them. Totally separate from relationship, the Mystery School of Aries Rising is to go at life as if doing it for the first time. It is what Christ meant when he said, "To enter the kingdom of heaven, you must enter as a small child." Learning about trust, innocence, and courage is the Aries path. However, on the relationship path the intent for Aries and Libra Rising is the same. The bottom line for partnership on this path is the relationship itself is the path to God.

CANCER/CAPRICORN AXIS

Throughout the ages, the Cancer/Capricorn path is the one most concerned with the seven generations to follow, and bringing a family in. Traditionally, it is a family path and a conservative path. However, now at the *Turning Of The Ages*, those with Cancer/Capricorn Rising are challenged to be revolutionaries and conservatives simultaneously. The challenge to be revolutionary is in the sense of totally disconnecting from what the previous culture believed was the content of family and community, but at the same time strengthen the commitment to nurture and care for the family in new and healthier ways.

Cancer/Capricorn also has a strong desire to become a responsible pillar of the community. A deep sense of caring and commitment to accomplish the goal of nurturing a family, and the community, is the primary purpose of any primary relationship on this path. If someone has Cancer or Capricorn rising today, it doesn't necessarily mean they are to be a mother or father and take care of a family. They are, however, the ones on the front lines for discovering new, healthier ways to create family and community. One key factor in accomplishing this goal is to find something to believe in and then be committed to it.

Capricorn Rising is here to participate in the creation of a new operating manual, and to be the emerging elders of a community. Cancer Rising is here to figure out what the new content of family will look like in the next age. Their job is to discover entirely new ways of creating family and roots. It means defining who your real family is, and being committed to them. The definition of nurturing and commitment from the perspective of Cancer, is to be committed to caring for the seed until it grows to what for it is maturity. It could be a literal child, or it could be anything else that takes a seed form.

The Pluto in Cancer generation, from 1912 to 1939, had marvelous ideals about family, security, commitment, and the seven generations to follow, but an all too common trait of that generation was Cancer overkill. The problem for many with Pluto in Cancer is they never let go, and the initiations to separate the children from the parents never took place.

The immature version of Cancer is found in the example of a mother who has a child and abandons it. Balance for Cancer is somewhere between complete abandonment and over possessiveness. This is about healthy commitment to the seed until it grows to maturity and then letting it go. If there is anything this culture currently needs, it's revision on a deep core level of how to do family.

Where in this world is it safe to not know anything? Where is it safe to be a child? I am defining child as when a person comes into the life not knowing anything. Even an enlightened master who decides to incarnate again comes in initially not remembering his past, not knowing anything. Most people don't think about this, but when they incarnate, there is just as much of a surrender and a letting go process, as there is when someone dies.

When people die they have to give it all up; same thing happens when they incarnate, they have to give it all up. At birth, a person cannot remember their pedigree, or their high attainments. They have to let go of it and come in innocent as a child. In today's world the big question is, where is it safe for the children? There is a growing awareness of the extreme dysfunctionalism of the family in our culture. Therefore, the grand project is to revise what family is, and to make it safe, at this *Turning Of The Ages*, for all children.

Many of us have been involved in some kind of a consciousness group, or New Age group. Almost without exception, it's not long before we discover even those groups are not safe places; it's not long before we discover what the agenda is. This is about a complete overhauling of the family and community systems that are concerned with creating a safe space for the children, including the inner child of adults. There are not any real experts on this as this is unexplored territory. At the ending of an age, or the *Turning Of The Ages*, the old operating manual is being replaced, and it is all up for grabs.

The Cancer/Capricorn axis has as its relationship intent to participate in a whole new formulation of what it is to be a householder. This axis includes taking on the responsibility of envisioning a totally new family and community structure and then to be committed to bringing it into a successful and thriving form for the generations to follow.

LEO/AQUARIUS AXIS

This is the most radical axis of the six. The healthy Leo/Aquarius says to their prospective partner, "I am really fine on my own and I don't need you." And the prospective partner says, "Yes, I know, and I am really fine on my own, and I don't need you either." Then at that moment a spark ignites between them and they say, "But wouldn't it be amazing if we chose to have this dynamic dance, because we can do it out of complete freedom and choice." They both recognize each other as masters; each perfectly capable of handling their own lives, but they choose to be together because they have found the most powerful empowering person they could find.

The Healthy Leo/Aquarius bottom line intent for relationship is to empower and promote each other's uniqueness and individuality. This is a path absolutely designed to break apart old versions of codependency or couple consciousness. The new emerging abstract horoscope for humanity has Aquarius Rising and Leo on the seventh house which means the new emerging paradigm for all relationship paths is Leo/Aquarius regardless of what a person's actual relationship path is.

People with Leo or Aquarius Rising have two ways to approach the relationship issue, depending on their previous addictions, and depending on where they are coming from in their past life themes. This path can feel scary until it is understood, and each person in the relationship has a sense of harmony and balance and sense of self-worth and self-love, meaning they do not need a partner to validate who they are. If the Leo/ Aquarius Rising person does not have a strong sense of self without a partner, they will continue choosing relationships with partners who bust them of those addictions.

If they are not addicted to old-style relationships, then often their job is to attract people into their lives who are, and then bust them. The other path already mentioned is when two fully realized beings choose to participate in a relationship together.

There is no rule here that says one axis cannot be with another one; although some are more logically designed to get along together than others. This is why it is so important to know what the relationship intent is. When a person has the Cancer/Capricorn axis and they are with someone who has the Sagittarius/Gemini axis, important negotiations need to occur for that combination to work. Otherwise they each wind up projecting their agenda onto the other person, creating frustration for both partners.

In some cases, a relationship not working is the greatest thing that can happen, because it gives rise to the necessity to do the sacred marriage. This is something we all must do eventually anyway because, ultimately, there isn't anyone else out there. Experiencing the lack of a relationship is one way to get the sacred marriage teachings. The relationship axis gives us very important clues about what our true intent for relationship is, and this information is invaluable for determining our true goals and desires in regard to the intimate relationships in our lives.

Crop circle found in Ox Drove, near Bowerchalke, Wiltshire, England in 2015
Photo by Steven Alexander

Appendix II

The Emerald Tablet
Translation and rendition of Dennis Hauck

"That which is Below corresponds to That which is Above, and That which is Above corresponds to That which is Below, to accomplish the miracles of the ONE THING. And just as all things have come from this ONE THING, through the meditation of ONE MIND, so do all created things originate from this ONE THING, through Transformation.

Its Father is the Sun, and its Mother the Moon. The Wind carries it in its belly, its nurse is the Earth. It is the origin of ALL, the consecration of the Universe, its inherent Strength is perfected, if it is turned into EARTH.

Separate the Earth from Fire, the subtle from the gross, gently and with great ingenuity. It rises from Earth to Heaven and descends again to Earth, thereby combining within ITSELF the powers of both the Above and Below.

Thus will you obtain the glory of the Whole Universe. All obscurity will be clear to you. This is the greatest force of all powers, because it overcomes every subtle thing and penetrates every solid thing.

In this way the UNIVERSE is created. From this comes many wondrous applications, because this is the PATTERN."

About the Creators of this Book

DANIEL GIAMARIO

Daniel Giamario is the Director of the Shamanic Astrology Mystery School and creator of the Shamanic Astrology Paradigm.

He joins together an academic background in Comparative Philosophy and Spirituality with teaching meditation in two worldwide organizations and extensive world travel. Daniel learned astrology in the late 1960s and was part of Dane Rudhyar's humanistic astrological movement in the 1970s. After a vision quest experience on Mt. Shasta in 1981 his astrological vision and spiritual path became more earth centered and a shamanically oriented astrology was conceived. For many years, his specialty has been connecting astrology to the night sky at secluded locations and sacred sites to directly experience "As Above, So Below." He has been a full time astrological consultant since 1984.

Shamanic Astrology has evolved as a rich blend of psychological, mythological, spiritual, and shamanistic elements, specifically designed to assist in the unfoldment of the individual's life purpose and in navigating this pivotal point of the "*Turning Of The Ages.*"

In the early 1990s, Daniel Giamario, with the help of Cayelin Castell, began the Shamanic Astrology Mystery School, a land based, nomadic, and virtual curriculum for training counseling and therapeutic professionals in the use of the most important astrological tools and techniques.

Daniel's first book, *The Shamanic Astrology Handbook*, is available and a variety of other Shamanic Astrology books are in development. He has written numerous articles for *Mountain Astrologer* magazine and other publications. In 2013 he authored the Shamanic Astrology Divination Card Deck, currently available from the Shamanic Astrology Mystery School. Over the last 30 years, Daniel traveled extensively, teaching workshops all over the country in over thirty locations. He is currently traveling less, except for some regularly scheduled events in the Shamanic Astrology Mystery School curriculum, work with the Renaissance of the Sacred Feminine organization, as well as creating and producing workshops in exotic locations, such as Callanish in Scotland, Bali, and the Philippines.

Daniel's twin passions are the growing of the Shamanic Astrology Mystery School's body of knowledge, as well as continued research in the answering of the question: "Who are we? And what the Hell Happened?"

Daniel lives with his wife Lynne, going back and forth between Southern Arizona, Hawaii and Southeast Asia. He is available for in person and phone consultations, lectures and workshops. Daniel Giamario is a lively and stimulating radio and television guest and has hosted his own radio show on the Seventh Wave Network and other networks over the years. Follow his activities on **http://shamanicastrology.com.**

ROY PURCELL

Photo by Beverly Purcell

Roy Purcell is the essential journeyer, seeking from birth and time immemorial to explore and understand his journey as it reflects our own. Having early opened the door by word and image into the depths of his subconscious, he taps into its endless reserve of the collective memory of the world, its history, beauty and destiny.

He grew up a shy oversensitive boy in a rural community of central Utah's Wasatch Range, where the mountains cradled him and the vastness of the western desert beckoned his spirit. Drawn into that desert as a young man, the mystic qualities of his nature were ignited. After completing military, religious and educational endeavors, he sought solitude where he learned to listen to his inner creative voice. His search for meaning led him into history, mythology, psychology and the honing of his creative skills in writing and fine art.

He became well-known for poignant watercolors and etchings of western history and landscapes. His interest in printmaking led him into worldwide projects culminating in the production of the (then) world's largest intaglio prints. He then retreated from public life to focus on personal and spiritual growth and the development and mastery of various painting styles and techniques.

Fortunately for the rest of us his driving need to express what he perceives has left a legacy of beauty and understanding marking him as a pertinent voice for our times. His work brings us to a clearer vision of the continuum of our past, present and future. From his pen and his brush come a multi-dimensional statement spoken with the sensitivity and beauty rarely seen in the annals of creativity. A forum for Roy's books and portfolios can be found at Purcell Galleries in Tubac, Arizona, ***www.purcellgalleries.com*** ~ 520.398.1600.

GAEL CHILSON

Gael Chilson, in 1999, was the third person to be certified as a Shamanic Astrologer by Daniel Giamario and what has become known as the Shamanic Astrology Mystery School. Gael became acquainted with Daniel in 1989 when she heard him speak, first for ASA and then in Tucson for the Tucson Astrologers' Guild (for whom Gael currently serves as president). Attending Daniel's astrological vision quest camps and night sky talks became an obsession Gael indulged whenever possible. "My dad introduced me to the stars with knowledge and a telescope when I was five. Daniel connected me to the night sky in such a way that I felt at home with it."

Born only four days apart, their lives have corresponded in interesting ways. Gael picked up her first book on astrology the same year as Daniel – and the same book by Dane Rudhyar as Daniel first picked. Gael has practiced astrology professionally since the early 1970s but only as one of several businesses. "Daniel's method of reading the astrology chart resonated with me and I have been using it ever since I learned it."

Gael lives on her family home she grew up on south of Tucson, Arizona. She has hosted many of the Shamanic Astrology Mystery School classes (five-day intensives) since 2003. On one of the hilltops of this family property, Gael erected a rudimentary stone circle. This is where the Shamanic Astrology Mystery School was given birth on December 23, 2007 as Jupiter with the Sun set in the west and Mars rose with the Full Moon in the east. Find her on the web at ***www.athomewiththestarsastrology.com.***

SHAMANIC ASTROLOGY RESOURCES

THE SHAMANIC ASTROLOGY MYSTERY SCHOOL
The Shamanic Astrology Mystery School is a 501(c)(3) non-profit educational organization offering transformational education exploring the magical link between the land and sky. Trainings include a shamanically oriented astrology with astronomy and cosmology classes. The School offers in-person and web-based courses. A comprehensive certification program is available. See: ***http://shamanicastrology.com*** for more information about the school and its resources.

LEARNING MORE ABOUT THE SHAMANIC ASTROLOGY PARADIGM
The Shamanic Astrology Handbook by Daniel Giamario with Cayelin Castell is available as an E-book from Amazon or can be ordered directly from: ***http://shamanicastrology.com***.

ORDERING THE CARD DECK
If you purchased this book independently of the Shamanic Astrology Divination Card Deck, the deck can also be ordered from ***http://shamanicastrology.com***.

CPSIA information can be obtained
at www.ICGtesting.com
Printed in the USA
FSOW03n0034290617
35591FS